D0214240

DS
128.1
.A 6
Aker
October 1973

DATE DUE

Laramie County Community College
Instructional Resources Center
Cheyenne, Wyoming 82001

DISCARD

OCTOBER
1973

OCTOBER

The
Arab-Israeli
War

1973

FRANK AKER

Introduction by

MAJ. GEN. GEORGE S. PATTON
U.S. ARMY (RET.)

D.C.C.C. LIBRARY DISCARD

Archon Books • 1985

© 1985 Frank Aker. All rights reserved
First published 1985 as an Archon Book,
an imprint of The Shoe String Press Inc.
Hamden, Connecticut 06514

Printed in the United States of America

The paper in this book meets the guidelines for permanence and
durability of the Committee on Production Guidelines for Book
Longevity of the Council on Library Resources.

Library of Congress Cataloging in Publication Data

Aker, Frank, 1946–
    October 1973.

    Bibliography: p.
    Includes index.
    1. Israel–Arab War, 1973. I. Title.
DS128.1.A6   1985   956'.048   85–751
    ISBN 0–208–02066–7 (alk. paper)

Dedicated to

Maj. Gen. John K. Singlaub,
U.S. Army (Ret.)

He, like many commanders in this book,
paid the price of being responsive to military realities
rather than political perceptions.

CONTENTS

ACKNOWLEDGMENTS

The author wishes to thank the following individuals, whose assistance was invaluable in producing this book: consultant on armored warfare, T. P. Schweider; editorial assistance, James Thorpe III and Carolyn Marsh; battle maps cartography, Dana F. Lombardy; tactical organization and equipment charts, Dana F. Lombardy; aircraft scale drawings, Jim Walls; battle tank scale drawings, Dave Haugh; missile boat scale drawings, Jim Walls. The "Israel and Occupied Territories" map is courtesy of the U.S. Army Command and General Staff College, reprinted by permission.

INTRODUCTION

The Yom Kippur War, which took place in October 1973, was the fifth in the history of the post-World War II Arab-Israeli conflict. This is the story of that war. In the pages which follow this introduction, the reader will surely absorb an evenhanded and accurate account of this important conflict.

My association with these events, and with those soldiers who participated in them, began in 1971, when I became assistant commandant of the Armor School at Fort Knox, Kentucky. During that assignment, which lasted over two years, I experienced frequent contact with many members of the Israeli Defense Forces who were destined to play major roles in the combat operations described herein. In 1978, as a guest of Maj. Gen. Moshe "Mussa" Peled, I was able to tour most of the battlefields involved. Old acquaintances were, of course, renewed with Generals Adan, Reshef, Golani, Thal, and Eytan, all of whom are mentioned in this book.

While it is certainly true that much has been recorded concerning this conflict, my own study has failed to uncover a more comprehensive treatment that is so readable as this one. The author's coverage is complete, to include the operations of the land, sea, and air forces of all combatants. He provides details of the background to the conflict and then moves right into the various operational phases from the 6 October Arab attacks on both the Suez and Golan Heights fronts to the uneasy Kissinger cease-fire, nineteen days later. Dr. Aker outlines the supporting roles of both the United States and the Soviet Union. He renders detailed treatment of the obstacles both nations faced while supporting their selected "candidates." Certain aspects of this support, especially as they relate to training to fight Soviet-sponsored forces in a future "unpleasantness," should, in my view, be of high interest to Western military staffs.

It is of extreme importance that those whose business involves the art of war (and, although no longer active, I proudly join that group) provide careful reflection on certain tactical and strategic messages which emerge in these pages. They are highlighted here.

This was conventional, nonnuclear war, conducted with a very high degree of intensity. In nineteen days of heavy fighting, over seven thousand men lost their lives. Four hundred and eighty-five aircraft and over sixteen hundred tanks were destroyed. These losses are double those sustained by Axis and British forces during the El Alamein battles of November 1942. Notwithstanding the advent of the individually launched antitank missiles which were used so effectively during the early Egyptian attacks, it seems that, once again, the tank continues to be in good health. Since all wars are based on the two ingredients of fire and maneuver, the tank combines both, which, together with its protective armor, permits it to close with and destroy the enemy. It is still the ultimate offensive weapon on the battlefield.

This war emphasized, once again, the perennial requirements for balance and continuous coordination of land, sea, and air efforts. In this context, however, we see a centralized Arab command and control system pitted against a decentralized Israeli structure. This latter doctrinal approach was able to capitalize on and respond to fleeting opportunities emerging periodically from a very fluid battlefield situation. The author's discussion of these characteristics is valuable. The requirements for infantry (in this case mechanized) continues to pertain. The ground-combat soldier is still needed.

The requirement for reliable battlefield intelligence endures. Here it must be remembered that the clever and prompt application of that intelligence is normally the real payoff, and a Vietnam War lesson once again emerges.

Although the foregoing are, to me, the principal Yom Kippur War lessons, there are certainly others which become clearly evident as the text moves along. In sum, there is much to be learned from these

pages. Remembering the words of Mao Tse Tung, "Reading is learning but applying it is also learning and the more important kind. . . ."

Frank Aker may be justly proud of the contribution he has made
toward that application.

Maj. Gen. George S. Patton, U.S. Army (Ret.)
Washington, D.C.
May 1983

1

BACKGROUND
TO WAR

THE HOSTILE NEIGHBORS

That aerospace technology has dramatically shrunk the time and space concepts of this planet is an unarguable fact. The territorial imperatives of one nation are never far beyond the scrutiny of another. Such considerations must be present in modern offensive or defensive tactical planning, and when territory under contest serves two belligerents as a common border, there exist localized peculiarities not found in global conflict. These latter conditions applied in the Yom Kippur War involving, primarily, Israel and the Arab states.*

The state of Israel arose out of a conflict between two peoples— Arab and Jewish—occupying the same general territory and unable to settle their differences within it. Following World War II, the British passed the Palestine problem to the United Nations, which partitioned it into separate Arab and Jewish states. The inequitable distribution of lands and resources provoked the Palestinian Arabs to war, but they were no match for the well-organized force of Jewish World War II veterans. The remnants of Arab lands were annexed by bordering Arab states who also came to suffer the destabilizing effects of over one million Arab refugees. Israel was thus born in

---

*The Arab-Israeli war of October 1973 is best known as the Yom Kippur War in the U.S., U.K., and Israel. The Arabs refer to it as the Ramadan War.

conflict and it has ever since had to remain on the alert because of oft-repeated threats that she would be annihilated.

The Arab threats and military preparedness became so flagrant in 1967 that the Israelis opted for a preemptive strike against their neighbors. That conflict became known as the Six-Day War, since that was the amount of time necessary to neutralize the military capabilities of the Arab states. The victory was so swift and so complete that serious doubts were cast on the fighting ability of Arab military personnel, no matter how well armed or trained. The amount of military equipment destroyed or captured by the Israelis was staggering.

The territorial outcome of the 1967 conflict was Israeli control of additional Arab lands. The expanded borders included the Golan Heights in the north (taken from Syria and commanding a view of the valleys of northern Israel and the road to Syria's capital, Damascus); the West Bank of the Jordan (taken from Jordan and including the Christian and Islamic temples of Jerusalem); and the Sinai Peninsula, over 20,000 square miles of Egyptian territory east of the Suez Canal. Arab humiliation was so great that the Arab states refused to negotiate any kind of postwar settlement. The stage was irrevocably set for another clash. The Six-Day War also had significant bearing on future Israeli military actions because of the questionable assumptions it fostered, among them the following:

- Israel is permanently superior to its Arab neighbor states both militarily and economically;
- The Arabs are incapable of joint political and military action;
- Israel enjoys the sympathy of most of the world in its "involuntary" struggle against the Arabs.[1]

The last assumption suggests why the Yom Kippur War cannot be viewed exclusively in a limited regional context. The belligerents, having fought the only modern desert war, possess knowledge and experience no other nation can equal; their strategy and tactics—the Yom Kippur War as military paradigm—must inevitably be the subject of intensive study. Beyond that, the war had global overtones. As Mohammed Hassenein Heykal, former editor of the Cairo newspaper Al Ahram, wrote, "The Middle East related to the essential higher strategy of any major international power, and, therefore, neither of the two international sides involved in the Middle East—the

Soviet Union and the United States—can afford to cede the region to the other nor retreat from it."[2] In the interval between the two major confrontations, it was pointed out that the recurrent debate over whether the great powers should "become" involved in the Middle East suggested an unhistorical view of the situation. The great powers *were* already involved.

In another sense, the Middle East offers a classic example of the mutually aggravating interaction of big-power rivalries and local conflicts. Big-power interventions, in the pursuit of rival interests, helped inflame and fuel the Arab-Israeli conflict and frustrate peace-making efforts. The prejudices and passions endemic to the region tended to draw the big powers into quarrels in which neither had any vital interest and into perilous postures of confrontation that both had every reason to fear and avoid.[3]

The surprise Israeli strike during the 1967 war had caught Egyptian planes conveniently parked, wingtip to wingtip; most of them were destroyed within three hours. The attacks were launched against nineteen airfields and gave the Israelis air supremacy for their annexation of the Sinai, where seven Egyptian divisions (two armored, five infantry) were put to rout, abandoning late-model Soviet tanks as they fled for the African side of the Suez. Thousands of troops were captured while wandering in the desert.[4]

The international repercussions from the Six-Day War influenced decisions on the use and deployment of armament as well as the overall strategy of the encounter six years later, in October of 1973.

PEACETIME DEPLOYMENT

Before that October, Israel assumed that, because of Arab obstinacy, Israel must rely wholly on "defensible borders"—the farther flung, the more defensible.[5] A "defensible border" with Syria meant Israeli occupation and eventual annexation of the Golan Heights.[6] The West Bank of the Jordan would probably continue under the progressive and peaceful occupation that allowed commercial traffic of Jordanian farmers across the Allenby Bridge.[7] The Sinai presented the most complex problems of defense and surveillance because of the length of Israeli supply lines and the potential power of the Arab nations to the west.

While the land acquired from Syria and Jordan expanded Israeli territory only slightly, it provided additional space for residents of the Jewish state. Such was not the case with the Sinai Peninsula. It is basically uninhabitable, and the southern end is made up of impassable mountainous terrain, with only one modern road traversing the salt marshes in the twenty miles between the northern end of the mountain range and the Mediterranean Sea. The strategic settlements in this vast expanse are coastal cities—Gaza, on the coast just fifty miles south of Israel's main port of Tel Aviv, and Sharm el Sheik, at the southern end of the peninsula, on the Red Sea. The latter guards the Strait of Tiran, a window on the Gulf of Aqaba and the outlet for Israel's only southern seaport, Eilat. Roads have been built through three mountain passes in the middle of the peninsula. If the northern coastal road is cut, these passes must be used to cross the Sinai.

Israel's relatively peaceful relations with Jordan rendered unnecessary extensive deployment of Israeli forces or construction of defensive installations, along the Jordanian border. The situation vis-à-vis Syria was much more precarious. Syria had lost one of its crucial sites for shelling northern Israeli settlements when it was driven off the Golan Heights. To prevent the Syrians from retaking the Golan Heights, Israel had taken the following steps: hamlets that once housed Arab communities were left deserted; Jewish colonization of the area centered around fortified settlements, which would serve as a deterrent to guerrillas; and a patchwork of antitank obstacles was built, including mine fields and a wide antitank ditch, a line of reinforced concrete bunkers, and fixed tank emplacements with interlocking fields of fire. Only four roads lead from this area into Israel.

The Sinai defensive deployment utilized terrain characteristics in conjunction with manmade deterrents. Massive sand ramparts were thrown up on the eastern bank of the Suez Canal, high enough to stop armored vehicles. The Israelis knew they had to maintain constant surveillance of the Egyptian side while not exposing themselves to the artillery barrages that became more frequent after 1969. In fact, however, Israeli losses on that border, between 1967 and 1973, matched the number of men lost there during the Six-Day War. To counter such problems, a series of fortifications was built a short distance from the sand ramparts. Built and rebuilt three times in the "peacetime" interval, becoming stronger and larger each time, this became known as the Bar-Lev Line, in honor of its creator, General Bar-Lev. The line acquired all the drawbacks of a static line of fortifications and took its place with the Maginot and Siegfried lines as defensive failures.[8] (In post–Yom Kippur War analysis, the Israeli Defense Force Headquarters staff argued whether the Bar-Lev Line could be ranked as more of a modern "trip-wire" defense concept.)

Bar-Lev personnel controlled another defensive device. Large oil tanks had been buried deep beneath the sand and connected to a network of nozzles that would spray a wall of flame against anyone trying to make a crossing over the canal.

In fact, the Bar-Lev Line was no line at all but three substantial components integrated into a single defense strategy. The first element consisted of fortresses: stone- and sand-reinforced bunkers from which to observe the enemy and slow down any substantial attack. The forts were built in relation to the sparse but vital road complex of that desert area: whoever controlled the roads would dominate the entire peninsula.

Buttressing the stationary elements were two additional components, armor and artillery. Israel could never hope to compete with Egyptian cannon—these were too numerous, sophisticated, and well protected—but Israeli artillery was designed to take an awesome toll of any Arab advance. Beyond that, the Israeli tank forces were at token strength. Their mission was to buy time, not win battles. It was never envisioned that there would be a major buildup of enemy armor west of the canal in the space of a few hours.

Israel spent over $90 million on the defenses immediately adjacent to the canal and another $150 million on road construction to protect and supply these installations. The most important of the roads were a pair running north and south parallel to the canal, one about five miles to the east and the other eighteen miles. The defense plan was to use the forward road for 155mm and 175mm heavy artillery, with the road just behind carrying ammunition, supplies, and reserves of armor.[9] The artillery range was such that, from the safety of the forward road, enemy concentrations on the west bank of the canal could be bombarded. In the absence of artillery, Israel expected tanks to fulfill this role.

The natural barriers of the land dictated Israel's other defensive deployments. Between the easternmost road and the Sinai mountain ridges, the land appears roughly triangular in shape: sixty-five miles from north to south and forty miles wide at its deepest spot, narrowing to twenty miles in the south. Here one encounters a complex tangle of scrub and dunes, sand ridges and wide plateaus, and scattered waterholes and treacherous pans of soft, impassable sand.

The Sinai's central mountain ridges were the site of Israel's electronic distant-early-warning system. On the summit of 2,500-foot-high Umm Hashibi, just south of the Gidi Pass, a network of sophisticated sensors scanned the desert, the Suez Canal, and even the Egyptian airfields a hundred miles away for any sign of hostile activity. Construction was begun in 1969 but had not been completed by October 1973. In full operation, this early-warning system would use ultramodern heat sensors to detect the blast of jet engines deep inside Egypt; infrared photo scopes to scan approach corridors that might be used by troops at night; seismic detectors mounted on towers or buried in the ground to detect vibrations caused by marching troops or rolling vehicles; and magnetic sensors to pick up the approach of metallic objects—weapons, artillery, or tanks. Much of this equipment was automatic, and fewer than a hundred people were required to operate it from a control center well in the rear of the actual installations.[10]

The period between the military confrontations has been accurately labeled "No Peace, No War."[11] But the between-war deployments of the Arab states had very few defensive aspects. The Israelis mounted offensive actions usually in retaliation for guerrilla attacks launched from Arab sanctuaries. Thus, Arab deployments had a threefold purpose; to harass and inhibit the construction of military installations on land taken in 1967; to frighten Israel into full-scale alerts that took place away from their regular jobs, further distorting the defense budget and causing loss of face with the nation's leaders; and, finally, to lull the Israelis into a false sense of security while its adversaries quietly prepared to attack.

Arab armament lost in the Six-Day War was replaced by the Soviets. In fact, that armament was modernized: for example, World

War II T-34 tanks were replaced with T-55s and the most modern Russian armored vehicle, the T-62 tank. Most important, in view of 1967 deficiencies, a complete air defense system was installed in both Egypt and Syria. Many of the critics of the ground forces of those two countries in the Six-Day War forgot that those forces were at the mercy of the unchallenged Israeli air power. The air defense systems included dummy installations that outnumbered the actual missile sites almost two to one.

Arab forces during this period conducted regularly scheduled maneuvers, well aware that such activities were plainly visible to the Israelis. These maneuvers were always planned so that observers would see them as defensive tactics. Not visible were the offensive practice sessions that were held at specially designated sites well away from the border area. These sites simulated the Israeli positions that might be attack targets, including a mock-up of the Suez Canal itself.

The devastation wrought on the Egyptian Air Force in 1967 was to be avoided by deploying the planes in Soviet-designed hangarettes. Each miniature hangar could hold two planes and was constructed with ten-foot-thick reinforced concrete walls, open on both ends to lessen bomb blast effects and easily camouflaged to look like sand hills.[12] Advanced Soviet bridging vehicles were assembled for an assault across the Suez.

COMBAT EFFECTIVENESS

The relative urgency of military preparations undertaken by the nations involved in the Middle East conflict dictated, to a great extent, the sizes of the active and reserve forces on both sides. Israel saw itself as the potential victim of a concerted Arab effort to destroy her. The original boundaries of the country had been established by a United Nations mandate, and the Israelis felt themselves required to do battle to gain or hold control of that land.

From an early slogan, "Israel delenda est" ("Israel must be destroyed"), to Nasser's statement at the Festival of Unity, in 1965, that "The meaning of Arab unity is the liquidation of Israel,"[13] the Israelis knew that they must remain alert. Thus every Israeli from the age of eighteen to fifty-five was trained as a soldier. Regular call-ups ensured that each individual was militarily competent, whether he was serving in a fighting unit or the Haga civil defense force.[14] With a population of about three million, the Israelis maintained an active duty force of 94,000, with a ready reserve estimated at 180,000. The military budget in 1973 was 20 percent of the nation's GNP.[15]

The unique relationship of the Israeli military establishment to the population—the fact that nearly everyone had standby military duties—was both a strength and a weakness. The close proximity of population centers to actual or potential battle areas made mobilization logistically easier. However, the close-knit character of such concentrations caused the reservist to be unusually conversant with the abilities of his commander; the tight loyalties that theoretically bind most military organizations were often lacking. Another factor inhibiting military proficiency was the requirement of mandatory retirement from regular army service at age forty-five. Many people at the command level turned to politics on retirement. When activated during an emergency, they often found it hard to forget the political implications of their military decisions.

The two major Arab combatants, Egypt and Syria, maintained standing armies of 260,000 and 120,000 respectively. Egyptian reserves numbered nearly 500,000, and Syrian 200,000. The military in both countries was basically made up of members of the ruling caste. However, the infusion of Soviet weaponry and training programs required significantly more manpower and thus became a kind of adult education program. An economic side effect was the employment of otherwise unemployed rural workers.[16] By 1973, Egypt's military budget was 25 percent of its GNP.

Aside from peacetime staffing, combat effectiveness may be broadly defined as those activities that keep a nation's forces at the highest level of combat readiness. The extensive activities of the Yom Kippur War combatants between 1967 and 1973 were designed to neutralize the opponent's offensive or defensive positions, to test new weapon effectiveness, and to provide intelligence.

Such exercises were also designed with two other purposes in mind. Real military preparedness was to be camouflaged behind what appeared to be maneuvers or exercises, and the adversary was to be goaded into useless defensive action. The rationale here was simple: to take countermeasures against a reserve or weapons-testing exercise was a quick way to lose popular support. Each call-up was disruptive to the normal life-style of every reservist and had far-reaching effects. Disruption ranked as more than a personal inconvenience: activating a large reserve force temporarily interrupted the normal flow of commercial activity that constituted each country's productive life. When such losses were added to the costs of activating and maintaining larger military force, the economic hazards bred by indiscriminate call-ups become apparent.

Egyptian intelligence learned of the building of the Bar-Lev Line early. Thus Egypt's activities were first designed to destroy the desert fortifications. Clashes resulted, and artillery duels across the Suez commenced after the Six-Day War as soon as Egypt's lost military hardware had been replaced. By 1969 these barrages had become so frequent and intense that the situation was described by UN Secretary General U Thant as open warfare.[17] Soon Egyptian artillery fire was augmented by commando strikes against the defenses east of the canal. During one brief period, Israel suffered thirty men killed and seventy wounded. Israeli historians came to refer to this as the War of Attrition. It included air strikes that wiped out the radar controlling most of Egypt's Soviet-supplied SAM-2 missile sites, and an amphibious landing in the Gulf of Suez.

In the latter operation, the Israelis, on 9 September 1969, disembarked six tanks and three armored personnel carriers, all Soviet-made spoils of the Six-Day War. Manned by a hundred and fifty Arabic-speaking Israelis in Egyptian uniforms, the armor destroyed three major radar stations and killed about a hundred and fifty Egyptian soldiers. Eight tanks rolled back on the landing craft ten hours later. The raiders had captured intact two of the latest Soviet tank, the T-62, which the Egyptians had just received, and the latest Soviet mobile antiaircraft radar set, the P-12.

Such combat measures, and the countermeasures they provoked, determined to a great extent the weapons with which the Yom Kippur War would be fought. Military intelligence garnered from these experiences was translated into requests to the major powers for more advanced weaponry to defeat that which had just been discovered. Israel began to be supplied with Phantom jet fighters and American Electronic Counter Measures (ECM) to detect the point at which a SAM-2 radar had locked onto an aircraft. Egypt then made a strong case for a more advanced fighter than the MIG-21 and better air defenses than could be provided by the SAM-2. These requests were answered—after protracted diplomatic infighting—and Egyptian pilots began training with the newer equipment over Russian terrain resembling the Sinai. A large contingent of Soviet technicians was dispatched to install late-model air defense equipment and to train Egyptians to operate it.

With the Soviet Union as a formidable supply source, the activities of Syria and Egypt could be coordinated into a master plan that amounted to the prelude to combat. The Syrians repeatedly moved large armored vehicle formations into open view on the plains west of Damascus. They were always in defensive deployments so the Israelis watching from the Golan Heights would consider them nonthreatening maneuvers. The plan was to switch quickly to offensive formations just before an attack. The Egyptians also stepped up such maneuvers west of the canal. As the time for attack approached, they ceased to return all their personnel to quarters each night. Troops left behind were hidden behind the high sand ramparts bordering the canal. This buildup became the spearhead of the first attack wave. The maneuvers also provided cover for the construction of an overland communications system that could not be jammed or monitored, as could radio transmissions.

Both sides in the Yom Kippur War relied on outside sources to supply and train their military forces. Both also sought help in surveillance of their adversary's activities. While intimate details are best uncovered by the interception of messages, infiltration, or other forms of personal observation, an accurate overview can be achieved through high-altitude overflights and observation satellites. Only the superpowers had such hardware.

How much information was passed on to the Middle East countries, and how much they used, will never be known. Israeli Prime Minister Golda Meir has been quoted as saying:

> I cannot imagine that Israel would again consent to any deal under which we would have to depend for our security on others. We are more intelligent than that. One does not have to be very sophisticated to come to the conclusion, after the bitter experience of twenty years, that the only people we can depend on for our security are ourselves.[18]

On his part, Egypt's war minister, General Ismail, stated:

My appraisal was that [Israel] possessed four basic advantages: its air superiority; its technological skill; its minute and efficient training; and its reliance upon quick aid from the United States, which would ensure . . . a continuous flow of supplies. This enemy also had his basic disadvantages. His lines of communication were long and extended to several fronts, which made them difficult to defend. His manpower resources do not permit heavy losses of life. His economic resources prevent him from accepting a long war. He is, moreover, an enemy who suffers the evils of wanton conceit.[19]

And so the die was cast.

DECISION TO FIGHT

The decision to commit a nation to war is rarely a precipitous act, nor is the decision unrelated to the social, economic, and political threads woven into the fabric of the nation's life. When Anwar Sadat assumed the Egyptian presidency in 1970, he was essentially a dove, more inclined to seek diplomatic rather than military solutions to his country's problems with Israel. The mood of the country reflected a desire to remove the stigma of cowardice and military ineptness left over from the Six-Day War.

There was also a desire to test in combat conditions the later-generation hardware Egypt now possessed. Pressure from the hawks in Egypt's highest councils brought Egypt and Israel to the brink of war in the spring of 1971. Sadat maintained command by explaining that he was not against fighting to regain the Sinai, but that it was a matter of timing. Mobilization activities began on both sides, removing any element of suprise, so an Egyptian thrust at this time would have proved too costly. While this explanation bought him the time he needed to explore diplomatic solutions, it also committed him to fight if his approach did not work.

At the risk of oversimplifying the diplomatic impasse, two expressions may be noted as typifying the problem. Israel's willingness to negotiate seemed to be targeted on "the reopening of the Suez Canal," while Egyptian reference to the "resolution of the Palestinian problem" was equally destined to prevent any meaningful dialogue from taking place. Egypt recognized that the canal could never be opened without the concurrence of the forces controlling each bank, but it had no intention of leaving the eastern side in Israeli hands. Indeed, Egypt had closed the canal to all traffic partly to attract world attention to the situation.

Resolving the Palestinian problem meant, to Israel, surrendering pre-1967 lands for the establishment of an Arab state. But Israel had spent twenty-five years fighting for survival and was in no way prepared to divide its territory so as to be better liked among the Arabs.

None of the quoted statements was made by a representative of one of these countries to a representative of the other. All such dialogue was carried on indirectly, generally through the American state department, speaking for Israel, and through Soviet leaders, speaking for the Arabs.

Other factors were at work. A pan-Arab philosophy that Sadat inherited from Nasser gave rise to the feeling that a multi-front attack against Israel could succeed. For Egypt to ignore other Arab states was impossible, and there was further pressure to move against Israel. King Faisal, of Saudi Arabia, a devout Moslem and an extremely important financial source, felt he should have free access to the Dome of the Rock, in Jerusalem, the third holiest place in Islam.[20] Syria's minister of defense, Maj. Gen. Mustafa Tlas, has been described as hating Israel with a maniacal fury. He had lobbied since 1970 for a two-front assault on the Jewish state.

Sadat's "Year of Decision," 1971, came and went. As the year passed and diplomacy proved ineffectual, the Egyptian leader stated publicly time after time that he might have to resort to armed conflict. By April of 1973, there was no more "might" about it.

"I can only conclude from what you say that you believe a resumption of hostilities is the only way out?" asked Arnaud de Borchgrave, of *Newsweek.*

"You are quite right," responded Sadat. "Everything in this country is now being mobilized in earnest for the resumption of the battle—which is now inevitable."[21]

Unfortunately, Sadat's previous warnings induced the people who should have believed him to write off such statements as mere rhetoric. The Soviets launched some very mild attempts to cool the situation, but they found that the hardest part of riding a tiger is trying to dismount. By the time of the *Newsweek* interview, a steady flow of Soviet weapons was making its way to Egypt and Syria. Egypt's General Ismail was made commander-in-chief of the armies of the so-called Federation of Arab Republics. In the final phase of preparation, Sadat won the limited cooperation of Jordan's King Hussein. The Jordanian leader did not want to join Egypt and Syria in attacking Israel but agreed to provide a third front, thereby tying down Israeli forces and preventing a flank attack through Jordan into southern Syria.

All Arab leaders deferred to Sadat to give the final order for the countdown. General Ismail had chosen the code name "Operation Badr" for the attack, which had a target date of 6 October. For Moslems, 6 October was a special day, marking the 1,350th anniversary of the Battle of Badr, which launched Mohammad's triumphal entry into Mecca and the subsequent spread of Islam. For Jews, 6 October was also a special day—Yom Kippur, the Day of Atonement, the holiest day in the Jewish calendar.

On 13 September, Israel gave Sadat the pretext he needed. Four Israeli jets were patrolling over the Mediterranean, extremely close to Syrian air space if not actually in it. Syrian MIGs scrambled to intercept. Israel sent up reinforcements. Before the battle was over, about thirteen MIGs had been shot down. The Syrian leader, Assad, called Sadat with the details. Sadat gave the countdown order that night.

Sadat had selected the moment with care. He was driven by the need to avoid playing the aggressor's role on the international stage. He was also deferring, in the fashion of the faithful Moslem, to the words of Mohammed: "Fight in the way of Allah against those who fight against you, but begin not hostilities. Lo! Allah does not love aggressors."[22]

2

OPENING MOVES

An optimum tactical position in war is to have an enemy surrounded by powerful forces. The Arabs held almost that situation at the start of the Yom Kippur War. Of the 265 miles of Israel's eastern land border, 225 miles are shared with Jordan and the remainder with Syria. A ninety-mile line runs south from Port Said to the Gulf of Suez, where Israel and Egypt are separated only by the canal. Approximately 250 miles lie between the Egyptian and Syrian frontiers.

The conquests of 1967 had given Israel direct access to the Red Sea and had doubled its Mediterranean coastline. Neither acquisition relieved military pressure on the major population centers. The positions of Egypt and Syria made a two-front defense obligatory. Israel was a geopolitical island.[1]

Israeli strategic thinking had taken into account the possibility of a defensive war on two fronts. The most obvious alternative was to take the initiative and strike at the more dangerous enemy first, then divert forces to the less critical front when the first problem was under control. The preemptive strike in the 1967 war was part of official Israeli doctrine that the conflict had to be carried to enemy territory from the very first moment. An enemy attack that penetrated into Israel and had to be contained before counterattack was possible was contrary to this doctrine.

As long as this doctrine endured, the main strength of the Israeli army could be held in reserve behind an air defense system that was permanently in a state of high alert. The military posture that assumed this doctrine to be operational did not take into account three factors of the Yom Kippur War: the failure of military intelligence; the blunt warning from the United States that she would withdraw all support if the Israelis struck first; and the existence of sixty-five miles of open desert between one attacking point and inhabited Israel. The second of these factors could not have been predicted in advance.

Problems inherent in a joint command, nominally under the direction of Egypt's Gen. Ahmed Ismail, became evident from the very outset. Arguments developed among the Arabs over the timing of the initial attack. The Syrians wanted to start early in the morning so that the Israelis would be facing a rising sun. The Egyptians protested that they would be facing the same slanting rays; they wanted to attack at sunset when the sun would be low in the western sky behind the attacking Egyptian forces. The discussion became absurd: each side tried to dissuade the other by pointing out that having the sun behind an armored force would be a disadvantage because the vehicles would be silhouetted on hilltops and would thus become easier targets for enemy gunners. Egypt's leadership asserted itself and selected 1800 hours (6 P.M.) as the attack time. A subsequent compromise avoided both the sunrise and sunset extremes, and 1400 hours was chosen. This adjustment of the starting time helped the Arab forces, because Israel had intercepted a message specifying the original time and, never learning of the change, had geared for certain attack at dusk instead of four hours earlier.

It is not suggested that the selection of a date and time for a coordinated Arab attack was based merely on the religious holidays of the countries involved and on the advantages of the sun's position. Months of planning preceded selection of a date that would provide adequate moonlight, mild currents in the canal, and decent weather on the Syrian front. On the basis of such data, and from political realities, the choice was narrowed to the date and hour that would fulfill various conditions.

It is not possible to establish whether and to what extent the Soviet Union encouraged the Egyptian and Syrian attack. Certain indications suggest that it did so: purely offensive weapons had been delivered along with the specialized equipment needed to cross the Suez Canal, and the first ships carrying war materials to replenish

Egyptian and Syrian arsenals reportedly sailed from Odessa even before the attack had been launched. But, for the time being, the evidence is incomplete. All that can be established with any certainty is that the Soviet Union had advance knowledge of the attack, did nothing to stop it, and, on the contrary, tried to spread the conflict.[2]

In retrospect, one thing seems clear: the objectives of the Yom Kippur assault. Egyptian leaders used the coordinated planning sessions to sell their allies on the concept of limited objectives vis-à-vis the idea of totally exterminating the state of Israel. Syria was to regain the Golan Heights and again stare down Israel's throat while removing the threat to its own national capital, Damascus. The West Bank would be returned to Jordan and would include a partitioned Palestine, with the Dome of the Rock open to Moslem pilgrims. Finally, Egypt would rule the Sinai once it held the seaport of Gaza, on the Mediterranean, and Sharm el Sheik, on the Red Sea at the mouth of the Gulf of Aqaba.

The main objective, then, was to recapture the lands lost to Israel in the Six-Day War. It seems entirely possible that two variations of this plan were never stated at the conference table. The Syrians privately suggested to some observers that, with the abundance of modern arms they possessed and because of the shorter distances from the frontier to the heart of Israel, she would easily sweep through the Jewish land and achieve total victory. On the other hand, the Egyptian leaders seemed more practical. Even if the military onslaught did not regain all of the lost territory, it would be a worthwhile effort if the stigma of cowardice and ineptness were removed from the Arab soldier, and if recaptured dignity made possible negotiations between equals rather than between the victorious Israeli and the vanquished Arab. Neither of these positions seems to have been made known to the other allies, but the temperaments of the two main Arab participants, and their subsequent actions, bear out the thesis.

STATIC DEFENSES, MOBILE MINDS

From the outset, the Yom Kippur War made it vividly clear that old military concepts no longer apply. The classic "line of battle" held by a corps or army has been replaced by the notion of an integrated unit called a combat team. The incredible mobility afforded these units, with their airlift capabilities and their tracked and armored cross-country vehicles, requires greater responsibility and flexibility at lower command echelons than was ever seen in relatively static, centrally controlled warfare. Also, while a coordinated attack uniting air power, artillery, and high-speed mechanized armor would take a fearsome toll in any given sector, it remains necessary to establish and sustain some type of physical occupation if an objective is to be considered won or successfully defended. The Middle East battles of 1973 often hinged on the ability of a local commander to take over and make strategic decisions. One side insisted on strong central control; the other did not.

Hostilities began at 1400 hours on Saturday, 6 October 1973, when six Syrian jets swept in over the Golan Heights and attacked the Israeli defense positions. Syrian artillery that had had six years in which to zero in on its targets began walking a barrage toward the Israeli tanks that were hastily assembling at their firing positions. Behind that curtain of fire, Syrian tanks advanced. Israeli gunners picked off the first enemy armor they saw and thought the ground attack had been blunted.

Nothing could have been less accurate. One of the more colorful reports on the intensity of the Golan attack came from an Australian serving as an UN observer in the "cease-fire" zone between the two countries. He reported seeing a formation of three hundred Syrian tanks rolling toward him, in four columns, two on each side of the road, turret hatches open and their commanders proudly at attention. "It wasn't like an attack," said the awed observer later, "it was like a parade ground demonstration."[3] Israeli defenders didn't believe that there were so many tanks in the world. The tanks were closely followed by bulldozers, some with mine flails, and armored personnel carriers.[4]

The attack took into account the small number of defenders manning the fortifications, the element of surprise, and the Israeli low state of alert. The Syrians hoped to prevent the arrival of Israeli reinforcements by a swift, deep penetration. At least seven hundred Syrian tanks went into action along the Golan front in that first wave, three Syrian divisions in all. Facing them were a hundred and seventy-six Israeli tanks—two understrength armored brigades.[5]

The Syrian border offered no buffer zone, and Israeli defensive positions were situated in a strip only seventeen miles wide, containing Jewish settlements. The defenders had no alternative but to stand and fight. One of the brigades faced overall odds of five to one, and, in local confrontations, as great as twelve to one. They mauled the first waves of Syrian tanks until they began to run low on ammunition. When they had to break from their emplacements they were picked off one by one.

The brigade began to suffer heavily. One battalion commander saw two hundred Syrian tanks bearing down on him. With no ammunition, he called for an artillery barrage on his position and the surrounding terrain, now crawling with attackers. The Syrian formation was scattered and the Israelis escaped, decimated. Sheer weight of numbers offset many such brave acts, so that the Israelis had lost the southern Golan by nightfall.[6] With better defensive positions and better coordination between ground and air, the brigade defending the northern sector held out that first day and survived to mount within a week the offensive that retook the Golan.

Meanwhile, the Egyptian attack against the Israeli positions in the Sinai was assuming the dimensions of all-out war. Led by low-flying MIGs and Sukhois, the Egyptians struck the Israeli airfields and launched an artillery barrage that involved two thousand guns.[7] Having broad, flat terrain to use as a staging area, the Egyptians were able to mount a blitzkrieg-like attack.

In the Sinai, the Israelis' lack of preparedness became painfully evident. To man the thirty-one strongpoints and twenty rear posts of the Bar-Lev Line at proper operational strength required at least a brigade of infantry, roughly four thousand men. On the day of the attack, one undersized battalion was on duty. Most of these troops were middle-aged businessmen on their last tour of duty before retiring from the reserves. Two hundred of the eight-hundred-man force had been given leaves for Yom Kippur. Their effectiveness was further impaired because the increased state of alert had not filtered down to the men in the field. Israeli forces in the Sinai were, thus, unaware that war was imminent.

The Egyptians began the 1973 war with three corps-sized formations, referred to as armies. The First Army, commanded by GHQ, deployed near Cairo; the Second Army, commanded by Maj. Gen. Saad Mamoun, was positioned between Port Said and the Great Bitter Lake; the Third Army, commanded by Maj. Gen. Abdel Moneim

Wassel, was located between the Great Bitter Lake and the Gulf of Suez. The Second and Third Armies were to assault and cross the canal with five divisions.

The Second Army's areas of responsibilities were:

- Brig. Faud Aziz Ghaly's Eighteenth Infantry Division: Port Said to El Firdan
- Brig. Husan Abu Saada's Second Infantry Division: El Firdan to Lake Timsah
- Brig. Adrab el Nabi Hafiz's Sixteenth Infantry Division: Lake Timsah to Great Bitter Lake

Two divisions were to stand in ready reserve:

- Brig. Irbahim Orabi's Twenty-first Armored Division
- Brig. Hasan al Abdel Latif's Twenty-third Mechanized Infantry Division

The Third Army's areas of responsibility were:

- Brig. Ahmen Zumur's Seventh Infantry Division: Great Bitter Lake to El Kubri
- Brig. Yussef Afifi's Nineteenth Infantry Division: El Kubri to Gulf of Suez

Standing in ready reserve was:

- Brig. Mohammed Abdel Kabil's Fourth Armored Division.

The coordinated Sinai campaign paid little attention to the men in the Bar-Lev bunkers. Air strikes were directed against the command and control system, while commando units were airlifted deep into the desert to seize strategic positions and prevent the advance of Israeli reserves. The softening-up process actually deterred immediate retaliation so that the canal bridging operation could begin.

The Suez Canal had been described as a "giant tank trap" and had been reinforced by sixty-foot-high sand ramparts on the eastern bank. The Israeli defense minister, Moshe Dayan, had predicted that any Egyptian attack across the canal would be finished in twenty-four hours. The Egyptian chief of staff, Lieutenant General Shazli, gave this alternative view:

The Suez Canal is a unique water barrier, due to the

steepness of the banks and their irregularity, which prevent amphibious vehicles from descending into or ascending out of the canal without a way being prepared. Dayan made his statement on the basis of calculations that our engineers would need twenty-four hours to establish bridges and that heavy equipment could not be got across the canal inside forty-eight hours—allowing time for the arrival at the front of Israeli armored reserves.[8]

"I had a theory that it would take them all night to set up the bridges," Dayan also noted, "and that we would be able to prevent this with our armor."[9]

Dayan's thinking was outdated. Newly developed Russian bridging equipment and an Egyptian engineer's innovative adaptation of a commercial device for breaching the ramparts made the defense minister's view a dangerous illusion.

TANKS VERSUS ENTRENCHED UNITS

The utility of entrenched defensive positions such as those held by the Israelis on the Golan Heights and in the Sinai had been discussed in an essay written by one of the geniuses of armored warfare. It was written in 1942, when Field Marshal Erwin Rommel was learning his subject in day-to-day combat. He wrote:

> Against a motorised and armored enemy, non-motorised infantry divisions are of value only in prepared positions. Once such positions have been pierced or outflanked and they are forced to retreat from them they become helpless victims of the motorised enemy. In extreme cases they can do no more than carry on in their positions to the last round.[10]

Since World War II, advancing weapons technology had rendered Rommel's comments less than accurate. Thirty-one years after the Afrika Korps, the foot soldier of the Sinai was not at the total mercy of a motorized enemy. He was equipped single-handedly to take on and destroy a fifty-ton tank.

However, the field marshal's remarks were an accurate description of the Israeli infantrymen manning static positions on the Golan Heights. The initial Arab attacks established heavy momentum, and the first lines of defense were inundated by waves of advancing enemy armor. Syrian tanks swept past scattered bunkers, manned by ten to fifteen men each, in a drive to capture the high ground. Because of Soviet arms supplies, Syria was fielding one of the most impressive collections of armor ever seen in the Middle East. This Syrian armor had the advantage of mobility and firepower vis-à-vis the Israeli infantry, yet Israel's air force dominated the Arab ground forces. First, however, Israeli pilots had to establish supremacy over the Syrian airmen and the surface-to-air missile launchers that accompanied the armored advance.

THE MOBILE RESPONSE

Analysis of this phase shows that Israeli planes defeated the Syrian mobile SAM-6 antiaircraft missile batteries protecting the armored ground forces. This was a bitter, bloody duel that saw 50 percent of the batteries destroyed and the remainder fleeing to defensive positions around Damascus. The retreat left the armored spearhead naked to Israeli air attack. Then the Israeli planes were able to blunt the thrust of the massive tank attack that penetrated almost all of the territory occupied in 1967 and approached the Jordan River and the Sea of Galilee. In the first four days of the war, the Israeli Air Force (IAF) was the only effective deterrent to the Syrian armored thrust.[11] It took that much time to mobilize, equip, and deliver reserves to the combat zone.

Israel's effort to open the skies over Golan, though successful, proved costly. Their planes were equipped with ECMs to jam the SAM-2 missiles, but the Israelis did not realize that the Arab air defenses had the latest Soviet antiaircraft missile, the SAM-6. The latter had never been used in combat before and no counter existed. Postwar intelligence examinations of damaged and burned-out portions of the SAM-6 described it as "unbelievably simple but extremely effective."[12]

In the first afternoon of the war, fighting under such conditions, Israel lost thirty Skyhawks and about ten Phantom jets over Golan, all to SAM-6s or to the devastating flak of the Soviet mobile ZSU-

23-4 SP antiaircraft batteries. The latter chewed up the Skyhawks if their pilots dropped to a low level in an effort to avoid the SAMs. Israeli losses were so heavy that air strikes were halted that first afternoon. The sophistication and effectiveness of the ground weapons had taken their toll, not the Syrian fighter planes.

Without air support there was no hope of stemming the Syrian advance through the Golan defenses, so flights had to be resumed. The Israeli pilots switched tactics; they began to attack from over Jordanian territory, to the south of the Syrian forces. Skimming in a low, northward curve, they hugged the ground contours until they burst over the Golan plateau, achieving a flanking approach to the Syrian armor and then departing toward Lebanon and the Mediterranean—without, it was hoped, ever passing over the deadly SAM sites.[13]

While the Syrians were committing every available aircraft to the Golan conflict, the Egyptian aerial effort was more restrained. General Ismail had repeatedly referred to the air superiority, technological capabilities, and meticulous training of the Israeli Air Force; thus he used only the air support he considered absolutely necessary.

The Egyptians committed two hundred fighters to the opening onslaught. Seven major air battles were fought on the southern front in the first six days of the war. The largest dogfight lasted fifty minutes and involved seventy Egyptian aircraft.[14]

THE BATTLES ARE JOINED

At first, the battles were joined between well-equipped, well-rehearsed Arab forces and the surprised skeleton crews manning the defense lines. Israelis not attending religious services were relaxing, doing laundry, and otherwise preparing to conclude their tour of duty. On the northern front, the narrow corridor of land brought the two forces face-to-face within moments of the original Syrian thrust.

A nineteen-year-old commander related that his unit got one of the early alerts. The unit began moving into position at noon. In the belief that it would not take long to stop any Arab tank attack, the men did not plan to break their religious fast. The next twenty hours could be described as the "nightmare of the Golan Heights." During that period, the ten-tank Israeli unit engaged in seven major battles. The best odds it ever had were even—tank for tank; usually they were outnumbered five or six to one. In the end, the unit counted over two hundred Syrian tanks destroyed. As Sunday dawned, the commander was wounded by a mortar hit on his tank hatch that disabled his vehicle. He left for the hospital knowing that the Syrians had paid dearly for his presence. His final report: "My Patton alone knocked out at least thirteen tanks."[15]

In the south, the Egyptians launched an attack force of some eight thousand men across the canal. They crossed in small dinghies, under cover of intense artillery and aerial bombardment. Lightweight ladders were used to scale the sand ramparts from which the attackers fanned out to engage the first lines of Israeli defenders. They rushed some of the well-fortified Israeli posts in a suicidal drive that resulted in heavy casualties. Some positions were ignored and by-passed in the search for Israeli tanks. Only one-third of the mechanized equipment that was to augment the Bar-Lev Line was in place; the remainder was being held in reserve because of a misunderstanding between Jerusalem and the field commander.

To the puzzlement of the Israelis in the Bar-Lev bunkers, many of the troops who came scrambling over the canal ramparts were carrying unusual equipment. Some had tubes over their shoulders; others were carrying "suitcases" either in their hands or strapped to their backs. These first troops did not try to capture the bunkers— that was the task of the second wave.

The Israeli situation became difficult. Two tank brigades were to offer crucial fire support for the Bar-Lev Line, with another in reserve, but the opposite occurred. Ironically, that blunder turned into an Israeli advantage, for the advance brigade became the victim of the strange equipment carried by the Arab invaders. The tubes were the launchers for a Soviet-built, rocket-propelled grenade. The suitcases contained the most sophisticated infantry antitank weapon yet seen in combat: the Sagger missile. Hidden by a sand dune, an Arab soldier simply opened the suitcase (which then became a launching platform), containing a guidance assembly like that used for flying model airplanes.[16] When fired, these missiles paid out fine electrical wires attached to the guidance controls. A bright orange glow from the tail of a missile gave the gunner the line of slight reference to direct it to the target. The first one-quarter mile of flight was needed to "gather" the missile on line, from which point it could be directed visually. It had an effective range of one mile.

One suitcase-carrying Egyptian squad destroyed eight Israeli tanks within ten minutes, later reporting: "The tanks accelerated to their maximum speed to avoid our rockets, but we could hit them in their weakest spots as long as they remained in range."[17]

While the combination of ground forces and artillery was engaging and neutralizing the Israeli defenses, the second phase of the Egyptian attack got underway. With reference to the devastating results of Israeli air strikes in the Six-Day War, and in keeping with General Ismail's respect for Israeli airmen, Egyptian reconquest of the Sinai was to progress only to the extent that adequate air defenses were operational. After the foot soldiers crossed the canal, equipment needed to provide these defenses began to move. In the ten-mile area east of the waterway, the latest generation of Soviet antitank and antiaircraft missiles were readied. The objective was to hold that ten-mile strip against counterattack by tanks and aircraft for a period of twelve to twenty-four hours while the main Egyptian force of tanks and heavy weapons crossed.

Israeli defensive calculations had not considered that the Arabs would have the weapons and equipment to achieve such objectives as defending a narrow strip of the Sinai against aerial and land attack, crossing the Suez Canal in less than forty-eight hours, and moving significant amounts of mechanized equipment over and through the massive ramparts which abutted the eastern banks of the waterway. Weaponry, equipment, and ingenuity, aided by defensive miscalculations, had carried the day for the Arabs.

Transporting heavy weapons across the Suez and then breaching the formidable ramparts could only take place if the east-bank foothold was tenable against Israeli counterattack. The mobility of the SAM missile batteries allowed the Egyptians to move quickly; an interlacing network of high-level and low-level missiles as well as flak guns and antitank weapons was established on the narrow strip east of the canal. Thus the Egyptians were able to hold off Israeli air strikes while they completed the major crossing. Their defense also included mobile radar to detect incoming flights.

The deterrent worked. First, it drove off attacking aircraft and then caused the Israelis to concentrate on the defensive network rather than on the bridgeheads. No estimate has been given on the number of missiles fired for each Israeli aircraft brought down, but witnesses said the skies over the canal were often filled with missiles long before any aircraft were in sight; most of the missiles appeared to explode harmlessly without ever approaching a target.[18]

The second technological development that affected the Egyptian timetable was an advanced type of Soviet PMP bridging vehicle. These were armored vehicles which carried one pontoon section on a hydraulically powered overhead frame. Operating procedure required the first vehicle to lower its pontoon section at the water's edge. After that had been secured, a second vehicle drove to the shore line and released the connecting section. When enough sections had been joined to bridge the waterway, the entire assembly was swung out until it touched the far shore. It took the Egyptians roughly half an hour to build a bridge that would span the canal and support heavy equipment. Two such bridges were built, under the cover of smoke, for each of the five Egyptian assault divisions. In addition, each division built a dummy bridge to draw Israeli aircraft into missile kill zones.

The final obstacles to an Egyptian Sinai invasion were the sand ramparts. Both sides had built up the natural embankments in six years. The embankments were too steep to climb, and there was no way around them. A passage had to be opened. In this case, the ingenious application of a civilian device became the Egyptian army's secret weapon. Using high-pressure jet hoses, with the canal as a water supply, holes were blasted in the sand walls in three to five hours. Bulldozers then widened the holes to permit passage by tanks and heavy weapons.

Israeli calculations on the time the enemy would require to cross the canal were in error by a multiple of four. The battle was joined in force much sooner than had been expected.

The Bar-Lev defenders of one bunker had some warning by military instinct that an attack was imminent: they knew there was probable danger when all of the "cover" activity stopped on the Egyptian side of the canal. Out of the ominous silence came the onslaught. When the bunker occupants realized that they had been bypassed, they started calling for assistance.

The first tanks came through a smokescreen that blinded the Israelis. Then the defenders learned they could not be rescued, because the Egyptians had airborne forces ten miles behind their positions. The next morning, a relief column was dispatched to rescue them but was ambushed by Egyptian commandos who had been rushed to the spot for that purpose.

The Israeli tanks in the immediate area were so thinly deployed that they were fighting a losing battle for survival. As tank reinforcements tried to reach them, they encountered heavy artillery barrages and the fire of the antitank weapons that had crossed the canal. The tankers could not see the aerial action, but they knew that Egyptian vehicles were having no difficulty moving freely through the desert. The first indication that the tide of battle might be changing was when Israeli planes swooped low over enemy concentrations. Soon Egyptian tanks and trucks were being blasted.

While the Egyptian advance appeared to have been slowed, the men in the bunkers could not yet be rescued. Israel controlled the air but did not have possession of the ground. Even so, sixty hours after the battle began, some survivors of the Bar-Lev escaped under cover of darkness. Dodging machine-gun fire and working their way through the debris of a giant tank battle, they were finally picked up by an Israeli tank and returned to a safe area.

MODERN INFANTRY AND AIR MOBILITY

Supersonic aircraft and giant armored vehicles command today's military headlines, but these are essentially tactical tools to be used in support of ground forces attempting to defend or conquer territory. Technology has radically altered the utilization of ground forces. The descriptive term "ground forces" refers solely to their area of combat and is no longer synonymous with "foot soldier"—one whose only means of transportation is his legs.

Logistical limitations that once restricted the effective range of ground forces have been essentially overcome. The use of airborne troops as an integral part of overall strategy began in World War II. The Egyptians applied those lessons expertly as they moved behind Israeli lines to seize vital terrain or natural bottlenecks.

Modern airborne tacticians prefer helicopters to parachutes. Helicopters provide greater concentrations of forces in the landing area, and the troops trained to regroup around their craft when the operation is complete.

The attacking Arabs dispatched crack commando units by heli-copter as soon as they felt the Israeli ground defenses sufficiently weakened by a combination of air strikes, artillery, and tank shelling. Israeli tank forces were unpleasantly surprised when they encoun-tered Egyptian infantry excellently organized and equipped for anti-tank warfare.

It should be remembered that not all armored vehicles are tanks. Russia had supplied the Arabs with a wide array of mechanized vehicles that increased the mobility of non-airborne infantry. They also had vehicles that were used to base offensive weapons (rocket launching pads), to carry specialized equipment (bridging sections), or to provide support services. Specialized vehicles have been de-signed and equipped with armorplate and offensive firepower to perform these vital tasks. The ratio of tanks to all other armored vehicles is generally one to one. At the start of the Yom Kippur War, the estimated Arab armored strength was: Egypt, 1,955 tanks to 2,000 armored vehicles,[19] and Syria, 1,300 tanks to 1,000 armored vehicles.[20]

In Arab strategy, the second or third wave of attacking tanks was usually accompanied by armored personnel carriers. Arab infan-trymen were trained to move toward an objective in coordination with the curtain of fire laid down by tanks. This strategy had some flaws. First, Israeli gunners could concentrate their fire on the per-sonnel vehicles as a fire deterrent to ground combat. Further, when a vehicle was damaged, survivors had to flee on foot through a field of fire. When the tanks were disabled, the personnel carriers stood little chance against an enemy tank; it became clearer that tanks should not operate alone in the van of attacking forces in open country but should play a fire support role as much as possible, concealing their positions.

The decision regarding vulnerability versus strike effectiveness was nowhere more meaningful than in the commitment of helicopter-transported commando units. When a helicopter is seriously dam-aged or destroyed, its occupants do not have the option of disem-barking and continuing to fight. When the vehicle loses its transport capability (that is, to remain airborne to its destination), those in-side are almost certain casualties.

Figures tell the story. Airlifted Syrian troops were a major factor in the recapture of the entrenchments on Mount Hermon, and Egypt dropped two thousand commandos in the area of the Sinai mountain passes to delay Israeli reinforcements. Most returned to their lines, mission accomplished.[21] But despite those successes, the toll of lives was heavy. Nearly fifty invading helicopters were shot down on both fronts because the Israeli gunners understood the significance of downing a troop-carrying aircraft.

Clearly, both the immensely increased firepower of the foot soldier and the radical changes in mobility had altered long-standing strategies and enlarged the infantryman's role by the time the Yom Kippur War started.

SUPPLY AND RESUPPLY

A shallow treatment of the Yom Kippur War might deal only with the combatants—their preparations, their motivation, their strategies, their victories, and their defeats. The immutable fact is that this conflict, which might have triggered a global war, was neither won nor lost on the sands of the Sinai and in the lava hills of Golan. The original arming of the Arabs and the Israelis and the continued logistical support provided by the two superpowers constitute key reasons why the conflict occurred; supply also affected the final outcome.

The negotiations between the Arab states and the Russians, like the Israeli-American armament talks, are a matter of historical record. While most of the world thought the period between the major conflicts of 1967 and 1973 was a time of relative stability in the Middle East, that was not the case. Those six years saw an escalation of the amounts and sophistication of arms shipped to that part of the world.

Each side was continually probing and testing the weapon capabilities of the other. The Arabs had been virtually stripped of all weapons in the Israeli onslaught of 1967; Russian resupply operations opened the period that Israel called the War of Attrition, an effort apparently designed to punish Israel's neighbors who offered refuge and support to the Palestine guerrillas. There were enough provocations to keep the Israeli raiders busy. The Egyptian-Russian justification for the continuing supply and upgrading of arms was that the debacle of 1967 had left Egypt and the Arab states with no bargaining power. They needed some military success to soften the Israeli-American position.

The vicious cycle began. When one side learned that the other had been supplied with more modern or more powerful equipment than it was getting, the supplying superpower was challenged to "cover that bet." Newer, more modern arms were invariably put into the supply line. Israel, however, had an advantage in the local arms race: It had enough of the arms manufacturing capability to have entered the arms export business, where her key products were Uzi submachine guns and Gabriel missiles.[22] The Gabriel was the first missile to be completely designed and built in Israel. Israeli scientists first worked in conjunction with the French in developing air-to-air, antitank, and tactical missiles.

While Israel's arms production developed some revenue and reduced the need to make purchases abroad, there are few bargains in the armament marketplace. While the small client states could pressure the superpowers for more and more arms, nothing was ever given free of charge. The national debts of the small countries are, in consequence, a direct result of these arms purchases. Whenever Egypt or Syria had available cash from one of their oil-producing allies, Russia insisted on C.O.D.

The superpowers were not at the instant beck and call of the small countries. The United States sought to keep Israel strong enough to defend itself, yet not so well armed that it would recklessly launch another preemptive strike against the Arab enemies. Thus an Israeli request often became tangled in state and/or defense department bureaucratic webs, and often the needed equipment was not delivered.

The Soviets had similar concerns. While they knew their client states would probably precipitate the conflict, the Russians were not inclined to provide the very latest and best equipment in the Soviet arsenal. Yet it remained a fact of political life that a battle lost in the Mideast was a direct reflection on the potential power of the supplier. The small states were not above exploiting the pride of the superpowers whenever they could.

After the losses suffered by the Arabs in the War of Attrition, Egypt began to receive the latest-model arms the Russians were willing to release. Egypt's Sadat and Syria's Assad virtually commuted to Moscow to negotiate for more arms as the decision to attack began to take shape. When the value of these shipments began to escalate wildly—to Syria, in 1972, $150 million, and for the first half of 1973, $185 million—the Russian ambassador in Damascus was quoted as saying: "These damned Syrians, they will take anything except advice."[23] The Arabs received expert training and on-site tactical assistance with the new equipment.

Israel's ultramodernization of her military hardware moved at a necessarily much slower pace. She had received some newer aircraft but was still flying many French Mirage jets. The most modern tanks she possessed were those captured from the Arabs in the Six-Day War and the War of Attrition. The main weapon in her tank force was the Patton M-48, considered obsolete by the American army.

The outbreak of the Yom Kippur War could have been predicted with accuracy if one could have simply closely observed the increased traffic in the arms supply channels. Once the two sides had reached a military standoff, the only reason for continued arms shipments would be to supply an attack—or a defense. The Soviet sea route to the Mideast is relatively short: from her major Black Sea port of Odessa, the Soviet Union's ships pass through the Turkish-held Hellespont and into the Aegean Sea, which joins the Mediterranean. Both Egypt and Syria have deepwater ports on the Mediterranean.

American surveillance recorded increased Soviet ship traffic to these seaports in late 1972 and early 1973. Next, Russian transport planes began jamming the air corridor through eastern Europe, refueling at Budapest or Prague and then flying on to Cairo or Damascus. The sea routes began the heavy resupply even before there were any Yom Kippur equipment losses.

When, because of faulty intelligence and because they had been forbidden to attack first, the Israelis caught the full brunt of those new Russian arms in Arab hands, the Americans realized that the matter had come down to cases: an overwhelming Arab victory loomed as a possibility. The United States began to resupply, and the result was one of the great logistical support efforts in all history. At the very least, it required a thirteen-hour flight from an east-coast American supply depot to Lod Airport, in Tel Aviv.[24]

Five days were needed to set all the machinery in motion—diplomatic, command, and operational—but then the flow began. Once started, this history-making operation fed supplies across

6,400 miles, with one refueling stop in the Azores. The planes of the U.S. Air Force Military Airlift Command (MAC) flew a zigzag course, respecting the air space over countries that disagreed with what was being done or wished to remain neutral. Not one item was lost or misplaced. Some 566 MAC flights delivered over 20,000 tons of war supplies, from handgun ammo to 50-ton tanks, from aircraft fuselages to whole helicopters.[25] The Israelis rushed this equipment into combat—in some cases, in three hours on the Golan front and in ten hours at the canal.

The massive American resupply effort, combined with the training, competence, and dedication of the Israeli fighting man, soon turned the tide of battle and decided the outcome of the Yom Kippur War.

3

MISSILES
GO TO WAR

In its first three days, the Yom Kippur War gave clear indication that it would be characterized by two features: massive tank battles and the widespread use of missiles. The tank battles ranked as the largest seen since World War II; missiles came into such general use that they played a dominant role in war for the first time.

TANKS ON THE GOLAN

Col. Ben Shoham, commander of the Israeli Barak brigade defending the southern Golan front, emerged as a central figure in the developing drama of the first two days, a drama that served as a harsh tactical school for both sides. The Barak brigade, numbering seventy-six tanks, sat along a line running roughly from the Kuneitra-Benot-Jacov axis south toward El Al and the Sea of Galilee.

The brigade had too much ground to cover. Syrian tank units arrived in two columns and divided into four main ones—classic deployment maneuvers designed either to scatter enemy forces by drawing them from cover or to make possible subsequent envelopment. Two of these columns moved against Shoham.

Missiles had not yet made their appearance when these battles were joined on the afternoon of the Day of Atonement, the tenth day of Ramadan. Ranged in the background, the missiles boasted various levels of mobility that, in some cases, determined whether they were to survive. The Syrian tanks, outnumbering Shoham's by five to one, and in some engagements by as many as twelve to one, advanced against prepared positions. An Israeli officer noted, "They flowed in like water, finding their way wherever they had the chance."[1]

Covered by a thunderous artillery barrage, the tanks slowly advanced through Israeli minefields and bridged a lengthy antitank ditch, suffering heavy losses.[2] Firing down lanes carefully plotted to cover probable lines of advance, well-trained Israeli tank gunners engaged in target practice. In one instance, thirteen attacking tanks were destroyed where they sat, thirteen abreast, deployed for maximum fire power. But the Syrian tanks kept coming, while the Israelis tried to hold firm.

From their particular Rubicon in this war—the cease-fire line—the Syrian tank units had seventeen miles to go to reach Israel, beyond the Golan Plateau. The distance was longer than it looked on the map. The Syrians took losses initially from the terrain as well as from the Israelis' tank guns: tank treads split and shattered on the rocky surface. But weight of numbers took its toll, and the defenders began to run out of ammunition. Faced with no alternative, and seeing the Syrian tanks fanning south in the late afternoon to outflank their positions, the defending units began to retreat. They became exposed and their losses mounted. At this juncture, an Israeli tank commander called down artillery fire on his own position.

In battle, as in so many areas of life, the slightest element may appear in retrospect to have had major importance. The magnification is real, not accidental. Israeli resistance on limited sectors of the southern Golan summed up their general defiance of both the enemy and the odds. The Syrians were delayed and may even have become confused. Certainly they appeared in the afternoon to lose some of the will to attack and press their advantages.

In the end the Syrians advanced only to El Al, the preestablished objective. Shoham's defense can thus be seen as a factor in the failure of the attacking forces to continue their drive. The Syrian tank commanders had shown initiative in penetrating to the lip of the Golan Heights, but they did not realize the brutal truth that Shoham's outgunned forces had been largely scattered by dusk of the first day. Little could have been done by the defenders to halt the Syrians' further determined thrusts. The way west lay open, perhaps as far as the Sea of Galilee.[3]

Shoham was killed about noon Sunday, the second day of the war, but he had utilized the preceding night to regroup what was left of his battered brigade. When the battle resumed that morning, he had received reinforcements—Sherman tanks crewed by reservists moving up to the southern Golan by the Tiberias Lake road.

By this time action had begotten reaction: missiles entered the picture as Israeli infantry reinforcements began firing SS-11 antitank missiles. And too, war in the third dimension—the air—had undergone adjustment and readjustment to take account of the Syrian missile defense and offense.

The initial Syrian tank assault on the Golan Heights necessitated heroic counterattacks from the air that in turn exposed an ingeniously planned missile defense network. That network has been described as "the first integrated missile system ever seen in combat."[4] In theory, at least, this defense system provided coverage for ground forces from hedgehopping level to more than 70,000 feet.

MISSILES IN THE SINAI

Egypt began a coordinated ground-air assault in the Sinai with strikes by some two hundred aircraft on Israeli air bases and communications centers at Bir el Thamada, Bir Gafgafa, and the forward sector headquarters at Tasa. The strikes seriously impeded Israel's response; with the Sinai airfields damaged, Israel had to launch counterstrikes from inside Israel. Air defense of the Golan front occupied many other aircraft—the bulk of the IAF—and resulted in the destruction of many of them.

Those Israeli aircraft that could be spared from the developing Golan battles included the canal bridges among their priority targets. Approaching at low level across the desert, the planes encountered heavy missile fire from the ground. As Egyptian Lieutenant General Shazli noted: "The enemy tried extreme low-flying tactics to get at the bridges but the SAM-7 rockets proved a magnificent success in bringing down the attackers."[5] Still, nearly all the dummy Soviet-made bridges were hit by the air attacks, some as many as five times. But according to Lieutenant General Shazli, their extremely flexible construction allowed for new sections to be added "in a matter, at times, of half an hour to an hour."[6]

Subsequent research indicated that Shazli's assessment of the SAM-7s exaggerated the truth: these infantry-borne missiles had effect only to a limited degree, as their explosive charges proved inadequate to the task of knocking the Israeli Phantoms, Mirages, and Skyhawks out of the sky. The track-mounted SAM-6s and the ZSU-23-4 SP batteries took a heavier toll.

Israeli air losses were heaviest in the first phase of the fighting, when pilots had to give close support before dealing adequately with the missile threat. But after this holding phase ended, the IAF could plan its support operations more selectively, and losses from missiles dropped considerably.[7]

Missiles had entered the Sinai picture almost from the opening minutes of the war, and they remained prominent even as Israel, "on the defensive for the first time since 1949,"[8] girded for the ground encounters to come.

The static nature of the Sinai defenses became a serious impediment in this situation: while Egyptian tanks rumbled across the hastily built bridges spanning the canal, over half of the two hundred and forty Israeli tanks in the Sinai were being immobilized or destroyed. Much of the initial damage was done by Egyptian tanks and bazooka-armed infantry crossing the canal. But the tank advance itself, taking Egyptian armor as much as ten miles into the desert in the drive aimed at the Mitla Pass, meant that much of Israel's other armor was outflanked.

By early Sunday, the dance of death involving mainly armor, artillery, and infantry was in full swing in the Sinai. Egypt had five hundred tanks across the ditch. Of the two roads that Israel had built parallel to the canal, one five miles back and the other some eighteen miles from the canal at the maximum, the former had been cut in places and the latter was threatened. Egyptian air strikes had destroyed nearly 40 percent of the artillery on which the Israeli command was depending for fire support. Egyptian commandos carried by helicopters were harassing the Israeli rear in a general effort to slow or stop the westward movement of reinforcements.

The pattern into which the Sinai battles fell indicates an initial heavy Egyptian push across the canal; withdrawal and consolidation of the attacking forces' hold on a strip along the eastern bank that averaged five miles in width; the start of a determined Israeli counterattack on 10 October; and the seesaw struggles that began with the ill-fated Egyptian effort on 14 October to reach and penetrate the Sinai's central north-south ridge.[9]

Each stage followed its predecessor, however, at the cost of cruelly wearing warfare. Neither side could guarantee victory at any given point; neither side could be certain that the effort put forth by troops would pay off in territory gained.

On Monday, 8 October, the third day of the war, Israeli forces mounted their first major armored counterattack. Here tactical missiles played a key role. Maj. Gen. Avraham (Bren) Adan, a leading Israeli tank tactician, commanded one of the strike divisions charged with carrying out the counterattack. As it turned out, Adan's division fought virtually alone, as the second strike unit under Maj. Gen. Ariel (Arik) Sharon failed to engage the enemy at all. Confused orders apparently lay behind this blunder.

Adan's plan, developed as a tactic following the 1967 war as a response to antitank missiles, called for a massed tank charge designed to break through enemy defenses. The charge was aimed at the Egyptian Second Division's bridgehead at El Firdan, which was pointed at the passes through the Sinai ridge. Adan had about a hundred tanks, many of them manned by crews newly arrived in the battle zone.

The attack, later named the Battle of El Firdan, has been called a "disasterous failure."[10] Kicking off with its units an estimated 90 percent ready, the strike force began its massed charged in midafternoon of 8 October. An officer serving under Adan recalled later what happened:

> We were advancing, and in the distance I saw specks dotted on the sand dunes. I couldn't make out what they were. As we got closer, I thought they looked like tree stumps. They were motionless and scattered across the terrain ahead of us. I got on the intercom and asked the tanks ahead what they made of it. One of my tank commanders radioed back: "My God, they're not tree stumps. They're men!" For a moment I couldn't understand. What were men doing standing out there—quite still—when we were advancing in our tanks toward them? Suddenly all hell broke loose. A barrage of missiles was being fired at us. Many of our tanks were hit. We had never come up against anything like this before....[11]

Faced by brave men with effective weapons, the Israeli counter-attack collapsed. In the ensuing hours and days, encouraged by success as much as the Israelis were discouraged by failure, the Egyptian forces redoubled their attempt to expand their bridgeheads and reduce the remaining defensive forts.

The latter operation proceeded slowly and methodically. The Egyptian effort was limited to consolidating their position instead of seizing the nearby passes. Egypt's commander-in-chief, Gen. Ahmed Ismail, defended the necessity of a slow advance, saying that he did not want troops going beyond the protective range of the SAM missiles across the canal.[12]

Well within this range, the troops turned to the destruction of the Bar-Lev forts. These were joined by radio loudspeaker-telephone systems, so as the Egyptian mop-up continued, the troopers manning one fort heard the screams of fellow troopers being roasted alive by flame-throwing tanks.[13]

MISSILE EMPLACEMENTS

In the highly mobile Yom Kippur War, the Israelis manned fixed positions on the two frontiers in question. Neither set of static emplacements served any very useful purpose, for mobility was the key to success. The Arab missiles were most effective when they kept moving; when they assumed semifixed or fixed positions, they began losing control of the situation.

Modern missile-launching devices are usually mounted on armored, self-propelled vehicles. The entire spectrum of missiles may be carried and fired this way, each from its own particular vehicle. Uncomplicated modifications can allow different types of launchers to be used for the same missile as tactical needs vary. Sagger anti-tank missiles were even mounted in banks of six—instead of being hand-carried by an infantryman—on special amphibious armored vehicles for the Suez campaign.

The devastating effects of these missiles became visible after Adan's 190th Armored Battalion ran afoul of the human "dots" in the desert on 8 October. Egyptian officers later reported that Egyptian tanks, and infantrymen armed with RPG-7 antitank weapons, waited as long as possible, then opened fire with guns, rockets, and missiles. The Egyptians said that thirty-four Israeli tanks were destroyed and a number of others captured intact. Most of the destroyed tanks were completely burned out. That effect was produced by the Soviet RPG-7 round, which burned its way into the tanks and then incinerated them from the inside.

The demolished hulks of both Israeli and Egyptian tanks at this site prompted one Egyptian infantry general to observe: "Generals everywhere are going to have to think very seriously about armored warfare and its future. The present generation of tanks is far too vulnerable to the new weapons now being used."[14] Thus, what was once considered the impregnable fortress of the desert appears to have fallen easy victim to modern weapons technology. The fact that the missiles are every bit as mobile as the tank, and becoming more powerful, may mark the Yom Kippur War as the last conflict in which classic tank battles occurred.

The increased firepower provided by the new missile-launching devices—be they hand-carried, moved by self-propelled vehicles, seaborne, or airborne—has altered long-standing tactical concepts, even beyond those applied to tank warfare. Because missiles and other modern weapons can devastate a "line of battle" troop concentration, it has become vital that ground forces be dispersed into smaller operational groups. No longer can corps and armies serve as the main or basic units of battle. They have been replaced by combat teams, units generally of regimental or brigade size with a combination of the firepower elements needed to operate as a complete unit in armored engagements.

The weaponry and support that make a combat team a viable military force have been perfected in the 1970s. New antitank and antiaircraft missiles are fired by ground troops. Radar and laser are being used to sight targets under the most adverse weather conditions. Two such weapons that figured prominently in the Yom Kippur War were the American TOW and the Russian Sagger antitank systems.

The American resupply and modernization of Israeli arms, launched in earnest once the war had started, included the second-generation TOW wire-guided unit. This weapon has nearly twice the effective range of the Russian model in addition to a more sophisticated tracking mechanism. The TOW is considerably more cumbersome, however. The "ease of handling" factor, most important to the infantryman who has to operate the weapon, often determines the length of time during which the man will be exposed to enemy fire. The general procedure in the Sinai was for the operator to remain hidden among the dunes until an enemy tank passed his position. He then quickly set up his missile launch base (the suitcase in which the Sagger had been carried, or a tripod stand for the TOW) and fired. Usually, more nerve than skill was needed, for it took the missile about ten seconds to reach its target. The operator had to remain in position during the missile's flight, and those ten seconds were an eternity to a man who had to concentrate on his objective while exposed to fire.

The one-man, one-tank destructive capability of the Arab infantryman was due to the new Russian Sagger missile. The Egyptians used missile-firing infantry exclusively to interdict Israeli tank advances through the desert. Infantrymen also comprised one of the lines of defense around the first antiaircraft batteries that were positioned in the Sinai before the heavy armor was in place. The Egyptians defended the new arrivals against ground attack with an outer ring of infantry, dug in with Sagger and RPG-7 antitank missiles, and an inner ring of tanks. Before Israel took command of the skies over the canal, these defenses allowed Egypt gradually to move its air umbrella westward to provide cover for the ground operation.[15]

The Yom Kippur War spotlighted a resurgence in the offensive and defensive uses of the infantry. Something similar had occurred earlier, in Indochina, because of the light and powerful armament the infantryman now carries.[16]

MISSILE TACTICS

The mobility and range of the launchers dictated the effective thrust of the ground forces. With the inclusion of missiles, the traditional artillery bombardment that precedes or accompanies a ground advance has become far more destructive. One of the photographers from the Yom Kippur War shows a column of Israeli armor and infantry advancing across the Sinai. The column is interlaced with mobile missile launchers, firing as they move. The irony is that the missiles are being fired from the Russian-made Katyushas (multibarreled rocket launchers) captured by the Israelis in the Six-Day War.

The perspective of military commanders regarding the necessity of missile cover for ground advances is the only explanation that has been offered for the Egyptian failure to continue their eastward movement to capture the passes in the mountains of the Sinai. That movement would have cut off Israeli resupply and reinforcement routes to the canal. The Egyptian high command has argued that the protective missile umbrella used by the Egyptian army was the key to the army's success in crossing the canal, but that it could not be moved forward quickly enough to allow immediate capture of the passes.[17] Assuming a totally defensive position vis-à-vis the air above them cost the Egyptians control of that air space and initiative on the ground, and finally turned the tide of battle.

The Israelis anticipated that the Arab air umbrella would be provided by missiles which required fixed sites, the SAM-2 and the SAM-3. The main disadvantage of these missiles was their relative immobility. Furthermore, most of their electronic secrets had been captured by the Americans in Vietnam, making countermeasures possible. Those two models were present, but a new model was also included.

The SAM-6, used by the Arabs in combat for the first time, gave Israeli pilots the most trouble. Mounted on a mobile launcher with an accompanying radar vehicle, the SAM-6 needs no fixed sites. With the two units working in tandem, the aircraft is detected by the targeting radar, which computes the missile's launching instructions. Another ground radar unit tracks the missile in mid-flight and guides it toward the target. A solid-rocket booster propels the missile to speeds of Mach 1.5, where a solid-fuel gas generator system is ignited to achieve cruise speeds of Mach 2.8.[18]

In the terminal phase of flight, the missile takes over the guidance itself, using a heat-seeking device that directs it toward the heat radiation from a jet plane's exhaust. In this type of application, it has a "slant range" of twenty-five miles. The SAM-6 is also used against low-flying aircraft, though its range is then reduced to fifteen miles and acquisition is more difficult because of radar "clutter" from the ground.[19]

ESCALATION

Evidence coming out of the Yom Kippur War indicated that the Egyptians and Syrians both had the Russian-made surface-to-surface land tactical missiles, the Frog-7, with a 37-mile range, and the Scud B, with a 175-mile range. Thus Israel was bracketed by at least two enemies who could reach any part of the country with missiles. Reports also listed Israel's major missile as the domestically made Jericho, which can be fired 275 miles—far enough to reach the capitals of all countries on its borders as well as other heavily populated cities in northeastern Egypt.[20]

These missiles achieved a sort of balance of terror. Syria used the Frog to a limited degree against Israeli settlements and provoked retaliation that could have escalated the conflict out of control. Egypt flaunted its heavy missiles and stockpiles of real or dummy nuclear warheads nearby to improve the bargaining position when the Sinai battlefield action turned against it.

Starting on Sunday, 7 October, Syria fired sixteen Frog missiles, or twice as many as Israeli intelligence believed the Syrians had— another indication of the volume of Russian support. The last rocket hit a large kibbutz before dawn, wrecking twelve buildings and causing over $250,000 worth of damage. Because of the safety precautions no one was hurt, but it was an indication of how vulnerable Israel's civilian population was to rocket warfare.

Israeli retribution had to be severe enough to threaten Syria's total fighting ability. It was recognized that such retaliation risked an uncontrollable escalation of the conflict, but it was felt that anything less would not stop the attacks.

At noon on the day the kibbutz was struck, three pairs of Israeli Phantoms swept in from the desert south of Damascus and opened up with rockets and cannon on the buildings of the Syrian Air Force and the Ministry of Defense, wreaking havoc inside both. Unfortunately, one of the strikes overshot and hit a residential street in the diplomatic quarter. There were civilian injuries and deaths, which the Israelis may or may not have wanted. Later that day, Moshe Dayan explained the situation:

> There were very basic considerations whether to take action against Damascus or not. We did it for the first time, and I don't know what the American reaction will be like. And their reaction is very important to us at all times and especially in this situation. There were two considerations: one of which was the use of the Frog missiles—because

once used, ground-to-ground missiles start to raise the possibility of civilian deaths. . . . It was decided to do it now as part of the over-all, supreme effort to get Syria out of the war.[21]

When the tide of battle turned against the Egyptians in the Suez Canal area, President Sadat boasted of missiles "on their pads, ready with one signal to be fired into the depths of Israel."[22] The boast hinted that these were Egyptian-made Zafir missiles. Western experts discounted the threat on the theory that the work done with ex-Nazi scientists was still incomplete. Americans had reason, however, to believe that Sadat meant to use Scud missiles.

U.S. reconnaissance had revealed that on a base a few miles east of Cairo, a battery of Soviet Scud missiles had been deployed. Ranged neatly alongside them were what some analysts held were the characteristic shapes of nuclear warheads.

Sadat scored his point, but the Americans had to let it be known that using such weapons would bring countermeasures sure to precipitate global war. The missiles and warheads had been openly displayed so that they might be seen. A leak was carefully placed in an international aerospace journal, acknowledging the sighting—without mentioning the warheads—and discussing the inadvisability of using missiles against civilian targets.

Now the two superpowers were once again at a standoff. Based on that sighting, the Israelis included the American Lance missile on the list of arms they needed from the United States. The near disaster caused by this missile "brinkmanship" allowed cooler heads to prevail and to confine the conflict to the Mideast.

4

WAR IN
THE AIR

PRELUDE

The opening skirmishes of the Yom Kippur War were fought in the air. They weren't initially related to the war but rather took place between 1967 and 1970. The viability of an Egyptian missile shield was established at this time, and the Israeli "breaking point"—that amount of overt activity which would trigger a preemptive retaliatory strike—was tested.

Immediately following the crushing defeat of the Six-Day War, Egypt's then President Nasser began moving Soviet-made SAM missiles into position west of the Suez Canal. Israeli defensive measures were restricted, because of increasing international pressure for a total cease-fire and because of Israeli reluctance to engage in aerial combat with MIGs that were—as the Israelis knew—manned by Russian pilots. As Egyptians were trained to assume the Suez patrol duties, more and more air battles were fought over these missile sites while the diplomatic search for peace continued.

From June 1967 until August 1970, the air losses in the Suez-Sinai area were approximately a hundred Egyptian aircraft to sixteen Israeli. But in the closing phase of that period—the six weeks before a cease-fire was signed in 1970—Israeli losses were running about even with the Egyptian. The totals were about half a dozen each.[1] The cease-fire was signed before the lesson had really sunk home in Israel that Egyptian pilots had become more capable than the easy victims of 1967. The cease-fire violations to follow also marked the genesis of the missile umbrella tactic that would play such an important role in October of 1973.

The well-known Israeli military manpower strategy—keeping a relatively small standing army backed by a well-trained ready reserve, with an air force in a constant state of high alert—was carefully considered in anticipating Israel's reaction to the Arabs' final preparations for attack. The plan was developed by the Egyptian chief of staff, Lt. Gen. Saad el Shazli, and was known as the "strategy of misdirection."

According to Shazli, the plan envisioned the possibility that Israel might guess what was afoot three days before the planned assault. If it were discovered, the hope seems to have been that Israel would launch a preemptive air strike, during which the Israeli aircraft would be lured into prepared "destruction zones" of hidden missile batteries.[2] Although the Israeli Air Force seems to have been more aware of the impending danger than other military commands, an eleventh-hour intelligence report suggested that there would be no attack, and so they did not strike the first blow.

Members of the Israeli high command have differed on the question of whether a preemptive strike was or was not authorized. Twenty-four hours before the attack began, Israel's chief of staff, Lt. Gen. David (Dado) Elazar, phoned the newly appointed air force commander, Maj. Gen. Benjamin Peled, and expressed his concerns. Elazar's staff testified at a postwar inquiry that Peled was asked how long it would take to get into a state of readiness for a quick strike. Peled reportedly replied that he would be in full operational readiness by the following morning. Elazar is supposed to have replied: "I give that order. Put the air force on a war footing."[3]

But sources close to Peled report a different version. They claim that Peled already had put the air force on a war footing. They claim that Peled wanted to prepare a preemptive strike as soon as he heard Elazar's account of the latest intelligence summary. Elazar, it is claimed, turned the request down. But he apparently did allow Peled to prepare for a preemptive strike the next day, to be launched if the signs of Egyptian preparation had by then become conclusive. The inquiry commission attributed the lack of action to the final line in the intelligence report, which reads: "... The probability that the Egyptians intend to resume hostilities is low."[4]

The prewar Israeli Air Force was made up primarily of French

Mirage 3s, American A-4 Skyhawks and F-4 Phantoms, and Israeli-built Barak fighters. The Mirage 3 was reengined with a General Electric J79 powerplant. The Barak was also powered with a J79, built under U.S. government license in Israel at the Bet Shemesh engine plant. These two planes were used exclusively as top cover air superiority fighters and accounted for most of the Arab MIGs destroyed in aerial combat. The F-4 shared the air superiority role when necessary, but it was used mainly as a strike aircraft against airfields and other hard targets as well as against strategic targets where longer range was required. The A-4 Skyhawk had the primary ground attack role and took the heaviest losses from SAMs and ZSU-23-4 SP quad-mounted 23mm flak guns.[5]

The prewar Arab air forces were larger than Israel's and practically all new. The Six-Day War had seen the annihilation of these air forces on the ground in one three-hour attack. Again, in January 1970, Israel bombed three Egyptian airfields, making Egypt's skies virtually open. Syria had suffered no such subsequent losses and could still use her former air bases[6] and her new MIG-21 fighters, forty of which were purchased as late as May 1973. The Egyptian experiences of '67 and '70 strengthened their belief that a large complement of medium-range bombers and fighter bombers—like the Jaguar, the Mirage, the Phantom, and the Sukhoi 20—was essential.[7] To avoid open invitation to destruction by the IAF, the new aircraft were hidden in underground hangars or combat-ready, camouflaged, concrete hangarettes of Soviet design. Published figures show that between these bases and those of Syria, the Arabs entered the war with eight hundred first-line planes (three times Israel's number) and received a hundred and seventy-two reinforcement planes from other Arab countries during the war.[8]

AIRBORNE

In a nation as small as Israel, the mobilization process is rather simple. Batteries of female soldiers telephone each air crew member: "This is not a call-up, but you are on alert. Do not leave your house. Repeat. Remain at home."

For most Israelis, midway through their fast, the Yom Kippur message was more baffling than ominous. The normal response, soldier-style, was that "the generals are playing games again." The Israeli is well inured to sudden call-ups—but why on Yom Kippur? Didn't the military pundits have anything better to do?[9]

Lt. Col. Baruch Cohen decided to break his fast in order to get some nourishment for the trip he was about to take. He felt doubly sacrilegious when he ordered his driver to take him on an inspection tour of the forward Sinai antiaircraft gun positions. Four minutes after the attack began, that driver was dead, killed by a strafing aircraft.

"They came so quickly I couldn't see them," recalled Lieutenant Pincas Oren, the base religious officer, who was conducting services when the delta-wing silhouettes flashed overhead:

> They flew low and hit hard. Several targets sustained damage. Our pilots were already airborne. Not only was it permitted to break our fast and fight, it was incumbent. It didn't matter anyway. By that time there were less than ten men in the synagogue. According to Jewish law, we couldn't pray anyway.[10]

A low-flying aircraft, with its guns blazing, is an awesome sight to the man on the ground. It was the same on the northern front as on the western. Sgt. Gary Salomon was stationed at a forward military post in the Golan Heights. He was startled out of his thoughts about the holidays at home.

> Twenty planes were coming at us. It all happened so fast, we didn't have a chance to properly identify them. They came in low, strafing our forward positions. I was scared. I had never been in real combat before. There was so much perspiration between my hands and the Uzi, I thought I was going to drop it.[11]

The Israeli Air Force got its first, toughest, and most decisive test in the first hours of the war, on the afternoon of 6 October, over the Golan Heights. Mobilization of the Israeli army had started less than twenty-four hours before the Arab attack and was still in its initial stages when the Syrian armor breakthrough on the Golan Heights, combined with the Egyptian crossing of the Suez Canal, threw the army into a panic and dislocation from which it never really recovered. Men and equipment were frantically shoved into the two front lines as fast as they reported. Few units went into battle with their own officers, equipment, or communications. This contributed to the unacceptably heavy ground losses in the early days of combat.

Until reserve Israeli armor could be properly marshaled and organized for a counterattack, the air force was the only effective military force opposing the Syrians in the Golan Heights area. Attacking the Syrian armor protected by the mobile SAM-6s and SAM-7s with an interlacing of ZSU-23-4 SP flak guns proved extremely costly. Approximately thirty-five to forty Israeli aircraft were lost that first afternoon.

The older model SAM-2s were routinely neutralized by Israeli ECM-jamming from helicopters and transports, and metal-foil chaff was dropped to confuse the tracking mechanisms. The latest model surface-to-air missile—the SAM-7 Strella—looked more dangerous than it was. Of the hundreds launched, only a few downed Israeli aircraft, even though many of the Strellas followed their heat-seeking guidance systems to score direct tailpipe hits. Apparently the Strella warhead was too small to cause lethal damage to a modern jet fighter structure, except for unusual hits. The SAM-6 scored some kills during the Golan battle, but its main contribution was to send the Israeli attack planes into their standard high-g, split-S evasive dive to the deck, where the ZSU-23s literally chewed them up.

In the face of the heavy missile fire, the Israeli Air Force switched its priority to attacking the batteries directly. The guidance radars became the primary targets. Both Skyhawks and Phantoms sprayed the SAM batteries with rockets, bombs, and cannon fire during a bitter four-day battle that destroyed half the Syrian SAMs in the first week and sent others fleeing toward Damascus to protect against rear-echelon air strikes. In retrospect, the SAM installations in the Golan area were not as effective as they might have been if the Soviet suppliers had included surveillance radar. When the Israelis learned of this flaw, they began dive-bombing the SAMs under the predictable curve of the climbing missile.

During the war on the Syrian front, the Israeli Air Force destroyed about a hundred and thirty Arab aircraft, both in the air and on the ground at Damascus airfields. But the Israeli Air Force also took its heaviest losses on this front—over eighty aircraft.

In the Sinai, having used artillery barrages to soften up the

Israelis and force them to seek cover, the Egyptians launched their first substantive air thrust. Egyptian planes dodged beneath the Israeli radar screen to destroy much of the Israeli Air Force of the Sinai sector before it became airborne. Antiaircraft guns and Hawk missile batteries took a heavy toll of the first Egyptian flights due to the high state of alert maintained by the IAF. Initially, this was the only effective response that the Arabs were to encounter.

When the first Israeli air defenders did approach the canal, they ran into what was described as a "wasteful" overuse of ground-to-air missiles. "It was like flying through hail," one Skyhawk pilot explained. "The skies were suddenly filled with SAMs and it required every bit of concentration to avoid being hit and still execute your mission."[12]

The excellence of the Israeli airman has been well established, but what of his Arab opponent? Since most Egyptian aircraft had been destroyed on the ground in 1967, there had been no opportunity at that time to judge their competence. In 1973, reporters covering the Egyptian side of the conflict saw a much higher confidence level among the pilots. The reason may have been that they had logged much more experience in the aircraft they were flying— particularly the Soviet-built MIG-21 fighter—in the off-on conflict between 1967 and 1973.

Egyptian military pilots still had a number of serious limitations. For example:

- Formal training programs—limited by Western standards— handicapped the pilots in air-to-air combat and especially in air-to-ground work. Air-to-air training was confined to Soviet-taught set-piece tactics, with little apparent effort to expand on these. The close air-support role had never been heavily stressed, and earlier MIG-21s were never really suited for this work anyway. The MIG-21Js, which had been delivered in quantity to Egypt in 1970, had greater close air-support potential because of more fuel capacity and four weapons pylons instead of two, but no apparent attempt was made to capitalize on those facts.
- Day-to-day flying was severely restricted in peacetime to conserve aircraft, thus preventing pilots from maintaining a finely honed combat readiness. Egyptian pilots did little night

flying, instrument flying, or flying over water, so they did not learn the finer touch that such flying develops. Comprehensive training programs did not exist to further refine the skills learned initially in formal flight training.

• Thorough technical comprehension of aircraft flown was limited by the fact that technical manuals were printed in English or Russian, neither of which was particularly well understood at such a high technical level by the Egyptian pilots. The result, according to one observer, was a basic lack of motivation on the pilot's part to gain a full understanding of his aircraft and its weapons systems.[13]

To make up for these shortcomings, Egyptian army organization was—and is—significantly different in two ways. First, air force pilots were assigned to each ground unit to serve as part of the forward air observer/controller system. Some question arose as to the effectiveness of this plan, as Egyptian pilots appeared to lack guidance on target priorities and often overlooked critical ground targets in favor of less important ones.

Second, Egypt built a massive antiaircraft air defense command. It is estimated that it made up one-fourth of Egypt's entire armed forces in terms of personnel, or approximately 75,000 men—three times larger than the air force. A unique aspect of this air defense force was that, although it was an army unit, it was commanded by an air force general, Mohammad Ali Fahmy.[14] Fahmy had attended the command staff meeting at which Sadat gave the order to attack. Still, the Egyptian Air Force and the air defense units combined destroyed only about thirty-five IAF planes in the Sinai.

Israeli air prowess provided a major reason why the Arab nations did not launch a three-nation ground attack. King Hussein of Jordan was committed to offer more than moral support to his neighbors, but he hedged his offer by agreeing to mount an offensive across the Jordan River when Syria had completely liberated the Golan Heights and the Egyptians had overrun the major desert passes that controlled the Sinai. As these conditions never did exist, he was spared sending his forces into the narrow rock defiles that approached the river, where Israeli armor could have wrought havoc.

More important, Hussein knew that Jordan's air force—a few Hawker Hunters—was no match for Israel's terrifying air power. Jordanian pilots could not handle a batch of F-104 Starfighters that the United States had supplied, and a consignment of simpler F-5s that had been promised had not yet entered service. The assessment of Hussein's chief of staff, Gen. Zeid bin Shaker, was that Jordan's armor might get as far as the hills overlooking the Holy City and might even inflict a lot of damage on the Israelis in the process. But then, without air cover, they would be wiped out in a bloody repeat of 1967. Hussein later fulfilled his commitment by sending an elite Jordanian tank brigade to help stem the Israeli advances in the southern Golan.[15]

Iraqi aircraft entered the war two days after it began. That Monday, 8 October, squadrons of Iraqi MIGs began operating over Golan. At least half a dozen were promptly shot down by Syrian SAM-6s because their IFF (Identification Friend or Foe) gear could not cope with the rapid switches in the SAM's radar wavelengths. Israeli pilots took another fifteen Iraqi planes out of the air in achieving control of the skies over Golan.

MISSILE UMBRELLA

For all the sophistication of rocket warfare, strong evidence suggests that many of the Israeli air-to-air kills were achieved with older-style armament. The Israelis succeeded in scoring hits on Arab fighter-bombers simply by sending up a large volume of fire. Numerous enemy aircraft, especially of older vintage, were reportedly brought down by Israelis firing small arms, mainly machine guns.

Standard antiaircraft batteries were also effective. On 6 October, a twenty-year-old 20mm gun instructor, Rami Kaplan, reported the attack of the first four Egyptian MIGs on his position east of the canal in these terms:

> They shot a brace of rockets at us from a height of about two hundred meters and the whole world turned black. I was the only regular Army man in the gun crew. The rest were reservists. I fired thirty shells at the lead MIG-17. It seemed to stop for a second, discharged another load of rockets and then began trailing smoke. A second later, it started moving erratically, like it thought it was a

helicopter. Then it jumped upward once and nosed into the sand. There was a great explosion. I felt great. No panic any longer.[16]

Such experiences raised serious doubts concerning the cost effectiveness of surface-to-air and air-to-air missiles. It certainly became evident that they had not completely negated the airplane as a combat weapon.

In 1973 the Israelis lost approximately 115 aircraft to all types of "surface-to-air" weapons. Less than half of these losses were attributed to missiles. The United States had similar experiences in Vietnam. Of 179 aircraft lost during a certain period, 168 were shot down by antiaircraft guns and only eleven by missiles.

Beyond that, it has been estimated that the Egyptian missile defenses along the Suez Canal were equivalent to the entire United States antiaircraft missile defenses deployed worldwide. For the cost of outfitting, training, manning, and supplying these installations, the Egyptians could have bought five times the number of aircraft that they destroyed.[17]

Confident of their ground-to-air missile superiority, the Egyptians were content to hold their air force in reserve, protected by hangarettes. The feeling was that once the Israeli planes were sufficiently mauled by the missile umbrella protecting the Egyptian forces, it would be time to carry the aerial war deeper into the Sinai and then to Israel itself. The Egyptians had not forgotten that during the War of Attrition, Israeli bombers had penetrated deep into Egypt, striking heavy blows at rear positions. The Egyptians looked forward to the opportunity to retaliate.

Meanwhile, elements of the Egyptian Air Force were ordered to keep pecking away at any Israeli counteroffensive. Along with the MIGs, they were also using giant TU-16 bombers as air-to-ground launching platforms for rockets aimed at Israeli installations throughout the peninsula.

The problem was that these modest Egyptian air attacks were not only sporadic, they were inconclusive. Israel thus regained and retained control over the Sinai skies. It was not the absent Egyptian airmen that posed a threat to Israeli pilots but the massive concentration of missile batteries on the eastern bank. The Arab-controlled west bank had an insufficient quantity of missiles to thwart any IAF attacks.

This limited commitment of Egyptian airmen to the Yom Kippur War was dictated by Gen. Ahmed Ismail, minister of war and commander-in-chief of Egyptian armed forces, who has on several occasions referred to the air and technological superiority, and the meticulous training, of the Israeli Air Force. There were only two times in the entire conflict that Egyptian planes ventured any distance from the missile umbrella.

In the opening hours of the war, Egyptian fighters hit Israeli positions in the Sinai as a deterrent to any counterattack while the bridgeheads were being established across the Suez and men and equipment were beginning to move eastward. Under the command of Gen. Hosni Mubarak, two hundred Egyptian aircraft were assigned the task of protecting the invading forces. At one time, seventy of these planes were engaged in a major air battle with the Israelis that lasted nearly an hour.

In the second incident, at the very end of the conflict, it was decided to use Egyptian planes to stop the Israelis from crossing the canal to the Egyptian side. By this time, many SAM batteries had been expended or silenced, so the situation amounted to pre-missile aerial warfare. Eighteen major air battles were fought, involving 2,500 sorties by Egyptian aircraft in seven days, a testimony of determination and heroism reminiscent of the English Spitfire pilots' performance during the Blitz.

Precise figures for aircraft lost during these two periods were never released. But it is known that Egypt lost a total of 242 aircraft, or thirty-eight percent of its initial force of combat planes during the Yom Kippur War.

THE DEFENSIVE POSTURE

While the opening Arab onslaught failed to cripple the IAF completely, the Israeli air arm was initially forced into a defensive posture. Unable to penetrate the integrated missile screen guarding the invasion forces, Israeli aircraft flew tight circles around their key installations, waiting for MIGs to attack. As the MIG-21s were taking losses, later-generation Soviet-built aircraft were introduced into combat.

This conflict may have strengthened doubts as to the combat

value of superfast aircraft. The Egyptians did fly some MIG-23s and MIG-25s in reconnaissance flights over Sinai. Whether supersonic planes, capable of Mach 3 as they are, are really suitable for anything else is doubtful. Operating at eighty thousand to ninety thousand feet, they are practically useless against ground forces. Descending to a lower altitude will allow for slower operating speed but will also seriously restrict maneuverability. Significantly, the F-4 Phantom, commonly regarded as the best all-around fighter in the world, was eighteen years old in 1973. Perhaps the only aspect of its performance which has not been greatly improved since it first flew is its speed.[18]

The measurable proof of the F-4s effectiveness in the hands of a well-trained and dedicated Israeli pilot was demonstrated not only by the totals of downed Arab planes but also by the fact that the Egyptian ground strategy was dictated by the extent of the missile umbrella that could be established. Though the IAF eventually pierced this shield, the original plans called for armor and infantry advances into the Sinai to move only with missile protection.

A prime morale factor for those flying combat missions is the knowledge that they will not be left to their own resources in the event that they might have to eject from a crippled plane. Israeli air rescue teams played a crucial role in locating downed pilots in Israeli-held territory and in areas controlled by the enemy. Large helicopters were used for these missions, because combat personnel were required if the machine was spotted by the enemy. A favorite Arab ambush technique was to wait for a rescue ship to land and then attempt to capture it intact. Several successful rescues were accomplished in the face of such tactics, heavy ground fire, and the ever-dangerous SAM batteries. The fact that Israel was prepared to risk an entire crew and complement of troops under such conditions provided a commentary on the extraordinarily high value the country placed on each airman's life. The Arabs, by contrast, had not established any air rescue units.

The heavy losses of men and equipment that resulted from the intensity of the opening hours of the war required that the combatants be immediately resupplied. The Soviets had opened their supply lines even before the firing began. Until the United States could be sure that Israel had neither provoked the conflict nor launched a preemptive strike, the American government was slow to respond to the requests for new equipment. When convinced that Israel's survival hung in the balance, however, America responded so massively that the results turned the tide of the war.

In replacing Israel's downed aircraft, the United States literally stripped some of its own active air force units. The F-4s, for example, came mainly from the U.S. Air Force fighter wing at Seymour Johnson Air Force Base, near Greensboro, North Carolina. The rest were lifted from the Sixth Fleet's two attack carriers in the Mediterranean, the USS *Independence* and the USS *Roosevelt*. The Skyhawk A-4s came partly from U.S. bases in Europe, but six had been raided from the U.S. Navy fighter weapons school at Miramar, California. Training came virtually to a standstill.[19] In all, forty Phantoms were sent to Israel, and at least six months would be required to replace these—a condition that was not generally known until long after hostilities ceased.

In the waning days of the war these replacement aircraft were seen over enemy positions along the Suez even before the Israeli modifications were installed. The Egyptian Third Army was raked ceaselessly, with tanks as prime targets. It was estimated that two-thirds of their tanks that crossed the canal were knocked out of action.

OUTCOME

The final aerial tally sheet for the Yom Kippur War would show that the Israeli Air Force, under the command of Maj. Gen. Benjamin Peled, proved as decisive in turning the tide of battle as it was during the 1967 Six-Day War. This remains true even though the IAF played a different and more complex role.

Analysis of the combat results of the eighteen-day conflict indicates that the Israeli Air Force achieved these major results:

- Blunted the thrust of the massive Syrian tank attack through the Golan Heights that had penetrated almost all of the 1967 occupied territory and was nearing the Jordan River and the Sea of Galilee. For the first four days of the war, the Israeli Air Force was the only effective force opposing the one thousand-tank Syrian armored thrust against the Golan Heights.

- Defeated the Syrian SAM antiaircraft missile batteries protecting the armored ground forces in a bitter, bloody duel that destroyed 50 percent of the batteries and forced the remainder to flee to fixed positions around Damascus, leaving the armored spearhead naked to Israeli air attacks.
- Neutralized the combined Arab air forces in a series of intense air-to-air battles that ranged from the Golan Heights to the Suez Canal. During these air battles, the Israeli Air Force destroyed a total of over three hundred and seventy Egyptian, Syrian, and Iraqi fighters, one Tupolev TU-16 Badger bomber, and about forty MI-8 helicopters. Only five Arab air strikes were able to penetrate the Israeli front lines. Combined Arab air forces had a 4 to 1 numerical superiority over the Israeli Air Force, and their loss ratio was 3.6 to 1.
- Destroyed a significant portion of the Syrian war economy in the first strategic bombing campaign in the long series of Mideast wars. The Israeli Air Force using McDonnell-Douglas F-4 Phantoms as its primary strike force, destroyed the only oil refinery in Syria, burned up half the oil storage capacity, wrecked port facilities through which Russian supplies were passing, and knocked out all major radio stations and power-generating facilities, literally plunging Syria into darkness for several nights.[20]

Israeli Air Force losses, throughout this activity, totaled about a hundred and fifteen aircraft. The losses included a dozen Dassault-Berguet Mirage 3s, about thirty-six F-4s, fifty-five A-4 Skyhawks, six Dassault Super Mystères, and six helicopters.

5

DESERT WARRIORS
AT SEA

When the 1973 war started, Israel had a cadre of experienced seamen composed of Jews from Palestine who had served in the British Royal Navy during World War II. These men, and others, acquired further experience between 1945 and 1947 smuggling immigrants into Palestine. At the same time, a small unit of Jewish frogmen, initially trained by the British during World War II, turned on their teachers. To break the British blockade of the Palestine coast, they sank two British coast-guard cutters in the harbor of Haifa and damaged or destroyed other naval vessels and shore installations.

This shadow navy was organized under the name Palym, the naval branch of the Palmach, the active full-time combat forces of the underground Haganah. The latter was under the control of the Jewish Agency, the unofficial government of the Jewish community in Palestine. Its main activities were smuggling arms to Palmach and delaying or interdicting arms shipments to the Arab states that were resisting the formation of the new country.

Many of the illegal immigrant ships that ran the British blockade were demilitarized surplus World War II vessels. These became the nucleus of the Israeli Navy upon the establishment of the state of Israel in 1948.[1]

The fledgling force became an important tactical weapon in the War of Independence. In late October 1948, when a large part of the Egyptian Army was cut off in Gaza, the Israeli Navy was ordered to complete the encirclement by cutting all sea communications. Two patrolling Israeli frigates sighted two Egyptian warships leaving Gaza and chased them back into port. An Israeli officer, Yochai Bin-Nun, later commander of the Israeli Navy, swam in and attached a home-made mine to the Egyptian flagship. The mine sank the ship and Bin-Nun was made a "Hero of Israel," one of less than a score so honored

The Egyptians lost another flagship to the Israelis. In October 1956, a converted British destroyer was assigned to bombard mili-tary and industrial targets near the city of Haifa. Two Israeli ships, with fighter-bomber support, were able to put the Egyptian warship out of service. Attempts to scuttle the ship failed and she surren-dered. The Israelis repaired the damage, renamed her the *Haifa*, and made her part of their navy.

In the ebb and flow of confrontations with its Arab neighbors, Israel came to understand that it had a very singular naval r   ...re-ment. As the amoun of land under its control grew, there were lu g, sparsely populated coastlines to patrol. The possibility of being in-volved in major naval battl s at sea was remote, and Israel knew that the requirements for a tactically oriented navy co ' ' not be met by remodeled castoffs of other navies.

A study of Western naval developr   ne early 1960s did not turn up a suitable vessel or weapons   n for Israeli purposes. Planning was undertaken to develop both, specifically tailored to concrete needs. The result was the *Saar-* (*Storm-*) class boat, armed with the medium-range Gabriel antiship guided missile.

How the Israelis finally added these items to their inventory offers a classic example of the confusing patterns of international diplomacy and of the almost childlike ruses and ploys that may be used to circumvent artificial barriers.

Working with the French naval industry, planning and construc-tion of the *Saar* class began shortly before the June 1967 War. France joined with other Western nations in declaring an embargo against Israel for the preemptive strike that appeared to start that conflict. Thus the twelve boats that had been built could not be delivered to the Israelis. However, Israeli crews were allowed to train on them in French waters!

The first acquisition occurred in 1969 and caused a minor dip-lomatic flurry. The Israelis literally stole seven boats that belonged to them, having paid for them. With the assistance of a tanker, they were able to run the embargo restrictions and get the seven boats to Israel. In late 1969, the other five were sold to a fictitious Scandinavian fishing company, only to show up in Israel later.

Aerial losses suffered by both sides in the period of undeclared war between 1967 and 1973 were discussed in the previous chapter. A parallel appeared in a naval incident that occurred at the start of this period, minor as regards the size of the loss but of major importance because it introduced a new chapter in naval warfare and also gave evidence of the ever-increasing Soviet naval presence in the eastern Mediterranean. At the same time that Egyptian artillery began harassing the Bar-Lev Line, the Israeli destroyer Eilat was hit and sunk by an Egyptian rocket vessel of Soviet origin near Port Said.[2]

By the start of the Yom Kippur War, the Israelis were as overmatched in comparative naval strength as they were in all other military categories. The overall ratio was nearly 2 to 1 in favor of the Arabs: Egypt had twelve conventional attack submarines and sixty fast patrol boats; Syria had twenty-five of the fast patrol boats; and Lebanon could put five more at Sadat's disposal. Against these hundred and two Arab warships, Israel had two conventional submarines and fifty-one fast attack boats.[3]

NAVAL STRATEGY

The territories being contested—the Sinai and the Golan Heights—occupied so much attention that one might logically have concluded that there was no other war. However, Egypt's strategists had considered all possible ways to get around Israeli fortifications and to reach the mountain passes through which any mass troop movements would have to pass. The brackish marshes bordering the Mediterranean coastline between Gaza and Port Said eliminated the possibility of an approach from the north. Thus Egyptian strategy relied on the army's ability to get inland from the south.

Egypt's naval strategy was the blockade. Israel became cut off from all seaborne traffic, notably tankers. The brevity of the war overshadows the significance of Egypt's decision. Had the war been extended, Israel could not have sustained itself solely by air deliveries. The threat to Israel is evidenced in the closing days of the war, when several attempts to break the blockade failed.

The southern blockade was echeloned. The Gulfs of Suez and Aqaba, which debouch on to the Red Sea at the southern end of the Sinai Peninsula, near the port city of Sharm el Sheik, were both closed by mine fields. The Bab el Mandeb Straits, entrance to the Red Sea, were in turn closed by Egyptian naval vessels.

The eastern Mediterranean had Egyptian naval patrols operating out of Israeli air and naval ranges. Egypt's military leaders also intended to land assault troops in the southern Sinai to attack radar installations, convoys, and small troop units, and to relay intelligence data to commanders crossing the canal.

Starting on the second day of the war, Israel launched its first truly offensive strikes south of the main battlefields. A flotilla of Gabriel-armed patrol boats encountered the Egyptian assault boats. The Israeli Navy now included a larger, faster, and better-armed patrol boat, the *Reshef*, to face Soviet-built *Osa*- and *Komar*-class Arab missile boats.[4] In this first encounter, the Israeli Navy detected and destroyed some of the loaded Egyptian assault boats trying to land commandos at Sharm el Sheik. Later, a second Egyptian naval force was intercepted and driven off.[5] Thus began the Israeli naval offensive that in approximately three days forced the Egyptian fleet of missile attack boats off the seas to stay bottled up in its berths for the remainder of the war.[6]

Syria's coastline on the Mediterranean begins some one hundred miles north of the nearest Israeli landfall. The intervening coast is the Lebanese shore. With the same reckless abandon that they had shown in the air with their new Russian equipment, the Syrians attempted to achieve a quick conquest at sea.

Describing a naval action occurring on 9 October in which his vessel allegedly sank five Syrian boats near Latakia, an Israeli naval commander related:

> We set sail in the afternoon, our objective being to seek and destroy enemy vessels in open water. By nightfall, we had encountered an enemy force, fairly close to shore, and on its way to the harbor.
>
> At about 2330, a Syrian torpedo boat was seen opposite Latakia. We launched a gun attack and sank her. At

the same time we made contact with a group of rapidly moving vessels.

Quickly concluding the battle with the torpedo boat, we took them on. They proved to be Syrian missile boats of the *Komar* type. A missile battle ensued.

We fired our missiles at them and they fired theirs back. We hit all three Syrian boats and emerged intact ourselves.

We then sighted a fourth enemy vessel—a minelayer—some distance off. We fired at it and hit it. Another of their vessels then tried to escape toward the shore. We destroyed it with cannon fire.[7]

Such actions pitted the Soviet Styx surface-to-surface missile against the much shorter range Israeli Gabriel missile. The advantage of superior range—twenty-five miles to about half that—should have been decisive. Nearly fifty Soviet missiles were fired, but not one hit was scored, probably because of Israeli electronic countermeasure equipment that could lock in on the high-trajectory Styx. On the other hand, at least eight *Osa-* and *Komar*-class craft were destroyed by Gabriel missiles skimming low over the water at great speed. In addition, at least three neutral merchant ships were caught in the sea battles and sunk. Additional Arab craft were sunk by gunfire from smaller motor missile boats. The Gabriel was so successful that the Arab navies ceased to leave port. As a result, Israeli boats bombarded coastal targets in Syria and Egypt at will.[8]

Sea action in the north was spectacular, with Syrian seamen displaying considerably more courage than skill. In the final days of the conflict, the surviving units attempted to fight from port, hidden among the commercial shipping. Almost all of the Syrian ships that were sunk here were hit by the Gabriel. The discriminative capabilities of the Gabriel were considered excellent, since only one merchant ship, and that Soviet, was sunk, while several others were lightly damaged in the Syrian port of Tartus. Israeli naval forces also effectively employed gunfire to destroy Syrian coastal petroleum and power installations.[9]

Against the Egyptians, later war operations were less spectacular but no less significant. By vigorous patrolling, the Israeli Navy kept minor units of the Egyptian Navy tied up in port. The Israelis became overconfident at reports of the numerous Egyptian missile boats that were sunk at sea by naval and air action during the first days of the war. Israel employed large frogmen units to attack and disrupt Port Said, Alexandria, and Baltim in the Mediterranean. The raids ended in disaster. Most of the frogmen were killed or captured, and two Saar-class boats were sunk. In the Gulf of Suez and the Red Sea, Israeli frogmen had better luck and did succeed in damaging a number of landing craft that were undergoing preparations for amphibious operations.[10]

SOVIET NAVAL INTERESTS

A distinctive factor characterized the naval combat of the Yom Kippur War. By contrast with the land engagements, the combatants were not the only military forces present. From a naval point of view, the Mediterranean–Black Sea area is one of the most heavily armed areas of the world; on, above, or below these fairly restricted waters, some one thousand fighting ships as well as over a thousand combat aircraft and a quarter of a million marines, sailors, and airmen may usually be found. In addition to the fighting ships, various nations had nearly a thousand other combat and auxiliary craft for mine warfare, amphibious operations, and supply service.[11] Nowhere else in the Mideast do such favorable conditions exist for an indiscriminate or accidental act that could produce an immediate big-power confrontation.

Each side in the ideological struggle between the United States and the Soviet, indeed, much of the world—has a vested interest in how the waterways that adjoin these nations are controlled and utilized. The most important of these is, of course, the Suez Canal.

In the aftermath of October 1973, attention once again focused on the strategic implications of the reopening of the canal. Prior to the conflict, the view was commonly held that the Suez Canal no longer had a vital role to play in international trade or military strategy. That reasoning was based on the fact that supertankers could not negotiate the waterway. Also, the petroleum products they carried would not be prohibitively costly (on a per unit basis) if they were to travel around the Cape of Good Hope. The vulnerability of the canal in the ages of ICBMs and supersonic aircraft made it seem of even less significance to the major powers—to all but one, that is.[12]

Control of the canal was a major, if not the principal, goal of the Soviets in their attempts to help determine the outcome of the conflict. This point is strongly emphasized by the fact that as early as 14 October the Russians were urging the Egyptians to accept an immediate cease-fire.[13] This was precisely at the time when the Egyptians had achieved control of the entire eastern bank of the canal and before Israeli countermeasures had been mounted to dislodge them and make the waterway a point of negotiation.

This analysis helps explain why the Soviet Union encouraged the Arab states to initiate hostilities despite the deterioration of relations between Egypt and the Russians during the preceding year. Even though military personnel were not officially attached to any of the fighting forces, the potential naval tinderbox in the eastern Mediterranean made the Soviet approach one of carefully calculated risk.

What positive goal did the Russians expect to achieve by their active, unreserved support of the hostilities? The shifting tides of global politics heightened the importance of the waterway in Soviet strategic thinking. The Suez Canal became vital to Russia if that nation was to change its overall naval strategy from a defensive to an offensive posture.[14]

The switch in Soviet naval planning seems to have taken place during the continuing hostilities in the Mideast. How much the change dictated the dispatch of heavy arms supplies to the Arabs may never be known. But it can now be seen that the change in Russian thinking made Arab control of the Suez imperative.

Previously the Russians had been content to hold a measure of control over the one major waterway nearest home, the Dardanelles. Now the Soviets appeared to be seeking control of, or at least influence over, the access gates leading to the world's oceans, preeminent among these the Suez Canal.[15] When Egypt closed the canal, it effectively terminated control of the waterway by Western powers, but it also added to Russia's naval problems.

While they were unable to use the Suez Canal, Soviet merchant and naval ships voyaging to East Africa and Asia, primarily North Vietnam, from Black Sea ports faced an additional nine-thousand-mile journey around the cape. This meant that the Soviet's lines of naval communication between the Mediterranean and the Indian and Pacific oceans were critically extended. The deterioration of Sino-Soviet relations during this period made a blocked Suez Canal even more critical.

It was little wonder that Soviet proposals for peace in the Middle East laid stress on an early reopening of the canal. The events of those years heightened the importance of the canal to Soviet strategy, even to the point where its forceful reopening by proxy was apparently worth the gamble of triggering a confrontation that might spread far beyond the Mideast.

The Soviet scenario failed. Egypt's President Sadat was not content with the early victories that gave him control of both banks. He wanted the entire Sinai, and his armies had scored such impressive victories that he was in no mood to accept limited gains just to please the Russians. Sadat believed that his navy could fight its way out of its ports and eventually effect an encircling amphibious landing at Sharm el Sheik. The Russians, for their part, had no intention of providing tactical support for such an operation. They had also come to respect the Israelis' efficiency in small-craft warfare. While the Soviets were still trying to convince Sadat that it was suicidal to pit Egyptian-manned Russian equipment against the Israeli missile boats, the point became academic. Israel broke Egypt's control of the canal and turned the tide of the Arab ground offensive.

Actually, naval power and efficiency made it possible for the Israelis to stop the Egyptian advance, stop the Syrians, and conclude the war as they did. These results, though, came not from the ships or guns of the Israeli Navy, but rather from the unique role played by the American Sixth Fleet.

THE SHIPS THE ARABS NEVER SAW

In *The Influence of Seapower*, Alfred T. Mahan wrote movingly of the far-distant, storm-beaten Royal Navy ships on which France's Grand Army never looked, yet which stood between Napoleon and dominion of the world.[16] So, too, did the ships of the U.S. Sixth Fleet remain far removed from the scene of combat while providing the knowledge and expertise that allowed the Israelis to acquire the equipment they needed to finish the war.

Publicity devoted to the day-to-day gains and losses in the air and on the ground gave impetus to a tendency to sum up the entire conflict in those terms. But, as noted earlier, a great deal more naval activity was involved in October of 1973 than the Israeli successes that have been described thus far. The eventual outcome of the war, and the avoidance of direct great-power participation in it, was brought about in part by the decisive and intelligent deployment of American sea power.

When hostilities broke out, the Sixth Fleet's striking force consisted of two carrier groups, one at either end of the Mediterranean. The eastern group in particular helped provide monitoring of increased Soviet air-transport activity to Egypt and Syria. It became apparent that the Soviets were replacing lost Arab equipment and that the Israelis would be defeated without similar support from the United States. The greatest airlift in history answered that call, but the application of American naval power had not been previously discussed.

The American response presented two problems, one general and one quite particular. The first was of command and control: the aerial supply route over the Mediterranean ran parallel to several thousand miles of hostile Arab airspace and was vulnerable to possible attack. This called for constant monitoring and precise command and control of all aircraft flying above the Sixth Fleet between the Strait of Gibraltar and the state of Israel.

The particular problem involved the logistics of ferrying short-range fighters the length of the Mediterranean. American bases in Europe were not available for aircraft that were destined for Israel because those governments feared an Arab reprisal in the form of an oil embargo. The presence of American naval power in that part of the world provided a viable alternative.

A comprehensive, interlocking network of PIRAZ (Positive Identification and Radar Advisory Zone) stations spanned the giant Phoenician waterway. American warships lay in place at the western opening, a hundred miles southeast of Sicily, while the eastern carrier group was headquartered aboard a command ship south of Crete. Extensive and secure communication facilities were available to pass and receive information to and from the aircraft in transit. The possibility of surprise attack on the transports and fighter-bombers had been eliminated because this network kept constant track of all aircraft in the vicinity, including any potentially hostile air contacts. Each flight was picked up as it approached Gibraltar and then handed down the long line, each ship assuming responsibility in turn until a safe landing was reported at Ben-Gurion Airport, in Tel Aviv.[17]

The logistical support problem for the Phantoms and Skyhawks was solved simultaneously. Two giant aircraft carriers occupied key positions, with the USS *Franklin D. Roosevelt* stationed south of Sicily and the eastern group including the USS *Independence*. These American airfields at sea were eminently suited to act as supply platforms for the ferrying fighters. The initial refueling took place near the Azores. Because the ground facilities there served as the single refueling stop for the transports, the fighters were either refueled on board the USS *Kennedy* or serviced in midair. From that point, they continued to the *Roosevelt* and on to the *Independence*, and finally to Tel Aviv.[18]

Though not one American naval vessel was involved in actual combat, the swiftness with which they were able to respond and the efficiency with which they filled this most unusual role contributed significantly to the resupply program for Israel. That may be the understatement of the entire war, for without the U.S. Sixth Fleet the Israelis might never have received the supplies that ultimately turned the tide of battle.

In addition, a Seventh Fleet task group, deployed in the Indian Ocean, played a supporting role for United States foreign policy during this critical time. Its purpose was to establish a U.S. naval presence that would serve to maintain freedom of transit in international waters throughout the area. It can be speculated that the Seventh Fleet's presence helped to provide a stabilizing influence during the Middle East negotiations.

LONG-RANGE IMPLICATIONS

Finally, it must be said that the U.S. naval command served other purposes. Its very presence deterred any outsider from joining the fray. Its role in the resupply operation was closely observed by the Russians and was an important factor in helping to spur Soviet pressure for an early negotiated peace. The American aircraft carrier efficiency under these conditions is considered one of the main reasons why the Russians in the mid-1970s started a carrier construction program. The carrier had earlier been conspicuously absent from Soviet fleets.

The Soviet Union did suffer maritime casualties during the war. Near the end of the second week of hostilities, she was landing tanks and SAM-6 batteries at the Egyptian port of Alexandria. The Israeli Navy was trying to make the sealift as dangerous as possible. In an Israeli skirmish with Arab ships protecting the port, a Soviet tanker was sunk. Russia warned of possible grave consequences for Israel, but with the American Sixth Fleet just over the horizon, nothing came of the threat.[19]

One notes an ever-increasing tendency on the part of military observers to compare the conflicts of the Mideast with the Spanish Civil War of the late '30s. More and more, the arena has become a testing ground for the weaponry and tactics developed by the superpowers. The Yom Kippur War was the first war in which naval forces on both sides used antiship missiles in large numbers. The results proved the destructive capabilities of small ships armed with such weapons. But it also proved that an antiship missile can be stopped by air defense weapons systems ranging from the most sophisticated antiaircraft missiles to World War II–vintage automatic guns.[20]

The small but tactically significant sea battles may have heralded a new era of naval warfare, and the simple statistics of Israeli successes speak for themselves. Questions are now being asked about the survivability of intermediate-size warships, such as destroyers, in the face of the proven guided-missile craft concept.

The case becomes even more compelling when guided-missile boats are supported by adequate tactical air cover.[21] When the Syrian Air Force was no longer a factor, the Israeli Navy was able to carry the sea battles past the coast of Lebanon directly to the Syrian ports. On their sea front, Egyptian warships apparently needed the same missile umbrella as did the land forces. When this was not available, Egypt's missile attack boats had to spend the greater part of the war in port.

6

THE HOLDING
ACTIONS

Tanks! The word usually conjures up images of a fleet of iron monsters churning up ground and spewing machine-gun bullets, with cannon belching fire and destruction. Most of the colorful leaders of World War II—men like Patton and Rommel—are associated with tank warfare. Indeed, the tank is considered the most significant single factor introduced into ground combat since the machine gun.

Tanks were first conceptualized as mobile pillboxes that would be moved forward slightly behind the first wave of infantry. Improvements in firepower and the development by the French of the rotating turret helped make the tank an offensive weapon in its own right. The use by the Germans of the tank in blitzkrieg tactics created a fluid battlefield in which positional warfare was virtually obsolete.

Tanks are demanding mistresses. They require constant care and upkeep. They will tolerate abuse only to a given point before making strange noises, or spewing oil, or throwing up a cloud of smoke, or simply malfunctioning for no apparent reason.

The commander of a tank is unique in the military. His exoskeleton, referred to as a tank, moves and destroys as his brain directs the nervous system supplied by the crew. The fact that the crewmen literally share a common mission and a common fate in combat increases the close-knit relationship and makes the tank commander's responsibilities singular. A seemingly minor mistake or oversight by one crew member may be fatal to the machine and all its occupants.

It is the "little things" that complicate fighting from a tank. The physical performance of each crewman's duties may not appear hard, but the small things add up. The gunner's role is to aim and fire the tank's main weapon. His range of vision is less than twenty degrees, and he operates from horribly cramped quarters.

Meanwhile, the driver's main problem is visibility. When not under fire, he has a poor perspective on the immediate terrain and must rely on the tank commander to direct him around impassable obstacles. Under fire, with the hatch closed, his vision is even more restricted, not to mention the problem of exiting if the tank is hit.

In combat, the loader works under almost inhuman conditions. He must have the correct shell ready to load, then load, then dodge the recoiling breach, and be ready again with a fresh round from some cramped section of the tank.

In battle, one basic proposition dominates today's tank tactics: No tank can carry enough armor to be safe all the time. A standard armor-piercing shell, fired at close range, will go through armor more than twice as thick as its own diameter. A tank firing a four-inch shell can, theoretically, at close range, pierce an eight-inch armor plate. It has been judged that heavier protection would so weigh down what is already a fifty-ton monster that it would lose effective mobility.

Enemy tanks are still a tank's greatest ground enemy—more so than artillery, more so at present than missiles. Only air power exceeds the opposing tank in destructive potential. This means that a well-armed tank that reaches the right tactical position can destroy any other tank—even one theoretically better than itself.

Each individual tank commander, and, more important, each person directing a squadron or more of tanks in battle, must learn one lesson: in an engagement, get off the first *accurate* round.

Just as the optimum alignment in naval warfare is to cross the enemy's T, tanks become most destructive when they emerge from cover to unleash their firepower on an unsuspecting enemy. Given the right terrain and covering noise from the enemy's tanks, such a tactical maneuver can be negotiated.

Because of the restricted visibility of the tank driver and gunner, it falls to the tank commander to direct his unit through the stages of advance that maneuver up to the moment when the first shots are fired. Because visibility through even the best of periscopes is strictly limited, commanders often ride as much as possible with their heads exposed.

Israeli tank commanders were trained to close their hatches only under heavy artillery bombardment. Some Syrian tanks were seen to enter combat with the commander's head and shoulders exposed above the hatch. That approach may have made for greater ease in directing the tank, but when the commander was killed or seriously wounded, his particular Armored Fighting Vehicle (AFV) was no longer contributing to the unit's assigned mission.

The Yom Kippur War's opening tank battles must be examined in light of such general considerations. For the Arab forces, these battles held the key to subsequent success or failure. For the Israelis, the battles ranked mainly as holding actions.

DEFENDING THE GOLAN FRONT

The 1973 conflict may have added two names to modern warfare's roster of colorful tank commanders. The first, Brigadier General Raphael (Raful) Eytan, surfaced in Israel's initial holding action on the Golan front. Here outnumbered Israeli tank units were deployed against massive Syrian armor. The second Israeli tank commander of note, Gen. Ariel (Arik) Sharon, led the counterattack in the south that put Israeli troops on the African continent.

The Israeli commander on the northern front, Maj. Gen. Yizhak Hoffi, decided on the first night of the war to place the defense of Golan in the hands of one man, Raful Eytan. The man matched the hour. A strong, taciturn man from a rural background, Eytan had been a career soldier except during a brief period when he returned to his farm. His silence made few close friends. He was not considered a strong tactician, but he stood unchallenged as one of Israel's most courageous fighters. The Israeli high command worried that he might endanger the men in his command. His record was replete with commendations, the highest possible praise in any army that does not award medals.

For all these contradictions, Hoffi had strong admiration for Eytan, whom he had first met as a fellow paratroop trainee. He needed someone on the spot who could make critical decisions to stem the Syrian advance until Israeli reserves could be activated, supplied, and brought to the front.

The initial Syrian attack was well planned. Three Syrian divisions were to attack across the Golan front: Brig. Omar Abrash's Seventh (mechanized) Infantry Division, in the northern sector; Col. Hassan Tourkmani's Ninth (mechanized) Infantry Division, in the central sector; and Brig. Ali Aslan's Fifth (mechanized) Infantry Division, in the southern sector. Two divisions were to stand in ready reserve: Col. Tewfig Jehne's First Armored Division and Brig. Mustafa Sharba's Third Armored Division. Though the Israelis deny it, their early defensive holding tactics in the Golan area were—because of Syrian planning and inadequate Israeli preparation—sporadic and ineffective. Individual Israeli tank squadrons moved gallantly forward, only to be blown apart. One nineteen-year-old Israeli tank commander described his experiences from a hospital bed in Safad:

> When we first heard of the possibility of an attack on Saturday, we got permission to break our fast, though many preferred to keep fasting.
>
> At 1400 we saw three Sukhois overhead. We rushed to our tanks and fired at them. An hour later we spread out in the terrain and, minutes later, a heavy bombardment began that made the ground tremble.[1]

One hour later, the first tank duels began in the northern Golan sector. When the Israelis had recovered from their initial mistakes, they acquitted themselves well against 3-to-1 odds; however, other Syrian waves would appear and double the Arab advantage. There was no nighttime that Saturday evening.

> The night turned into day, lit by phosphorus shells and explosions that made one hell of a racket. Our shooting was accurate, since we saw one Syrian tank after another burst into flames. Their whole lineup was one sea of flames.
>
> But ours got hit too. Several of our tanks had caught fire and the men jumped out....[2]

Fatique took its inevitable toll. At dawn the Israelis overcame a ten-tank Syrian company, taking eight of them head-on and knocking out the two that were attempting a flanking action.

> Then we saw a column of about fifty Syrian tanks and

armored vehicles five kilometers away and coming nearer. We stopped the first wave of that column, but the others, and enemy mortars, poured shells on us. One landed on the lid of my tank and wounded me and the wireless operator, who lost consciousness. They put us in another tank and took us to the hospital.[3]

Raful Eytan's division was to reduce these losses while yielding as little ground as possible. The commander's subtle intelligence became apparent as he directed that first night's defense. Instead of dashing about, an all-conquering hero present for each enemy encounter, Eytan set up a central command post. From that post he could direct his two brigade commanders and move his outnumbered armor into positions where they could inflict the greatest damage with minimal losses. Ironically, the Syrians had Eytan's command post, an underground bunker at Naffak, surrounded that first night, yet they did not realize that one of their tanks was less than thirty yards from the man who was translating field reports into measurements of Syrian weaknesses. In consequence, Eytan achieved devastating results by the adroit way in which he moved Israeli armor against the enemy.

As noted earlier, the southern sector of the Golan front was quiet that night. The Syrians, satisfied with their gains, awaited further orders. That was just as well, because the Israeli defenders in that sector had been badly battered and needed a break in the action, as well as darkness, to regroup their remaining operational vehicles.

MOBILE TACTICS

Raful Eytan's northern Seventh Armored brigade commander, Col. Janos Avigdor, was getting no rest. The Syrians were attempting to consolidate their positions so they could control one of the four major approaches to northern Israel. Thus, Syrian units concentrated their advance on the Golan's limited road net.

A decision was made: Avigdor's force would be split into two combat teams and moved into the rocky terrain adjoining the roads. From here, the Syrians could be harassed and picked off.

The choreography of the first-night battle will be recorded in the annals of classic tank warfare. The key tactic was to keep moving.

Israeli tanks wheeled from north to south and back again, many times crossing roads at right angles to heavy Syrian formations. After inflicting substantial damage with a flanking attack, the Israelis would disappear. Then the Syrians would see a lone Israeli tank peering around a roadside hill. The Syrians would chase the tank into a trap and be ambushed.

Where no natural cover was available, Avigdor created it. He had a squad of bulldozers that threw up earth ramparts for his tanks to hide behind. After the battle, one such rampart outside Kuneitra bore mute witness to the intensity of the struggle: behind it were four burned-out Israeli tanks; in front of it were twenty-six shattered Syrian ones.[4]

Wars, as Winston Churchill observed, are won by either slaughter or maneuver. Which form any particular war assumes depends on generalship and a variety of technological, psychological, and social factors.[5] The inflexibility of the Syrian command, one such factor, played into the hands of the Israeli defenders that first night. Had the Syrians temporarily set aside their main objectives and sought out their tormentors, the Israelis would have been overwhelmed by sheer weight of numbers. By staying on the roads and attempting to move constantly westward, the Syrian attackers set a pattern of predictability that allowed Eytan to direct combat teams in and out of the Arab formations at times and places that were most advantageous to him.

Rigidity of Russian training prevented the Syrians from deviating from the basic battle plan. The same rigidity actually multiplied the effective strength of the defending forces. All through the night, in carefully timed sequence, groups of Israeli tanks slipped through the blockading Syrians back to Naffak to refuel and rearm while the crews snatched a meal. Then it was back to battle, back to the roadblocks, the split-second ambushes, the desperate rescues, the harrying.[6]

Parenthetically, it should be noted that the equipment being used by the opposing sides had much to do with the Israeli success. Though the designers and manufacturers of the British, American, and Soviet tanks could not have had the undulating landscape of the Golan specifically in mind, the Israelis possessed superior equipment for this kind of cat-and-mouse warfare. The chief tactic was to approach enemy positions without being detected. Because the Israeli tanks could depress their guns 10 degrees below horizontal, they could stay below the crest of a hill and still fire down the far slope.

On Soviet tanks, by contrast, gun barrels could be lowered only 4 degrees from the horizontal. This meant that the tanks had to be brought up nearer the top of an incline before the target came into the gunsights.

By Sunday, 7 October, Israel had decided to make its major effort in the north. The Golan's proximity to her population centers, and terrain that offered fewer good defensive positions from which to conduct a holding action, had much to do with the decision. Also, Syria seemed initially to be the more dangerous enemy.

The first Israeli reservists readied for combat were sent to the Golan front to be used in stemming the Syrian advance. They were equipped with obsolete World War II Sherman tanks, undergunned and inadequately armored. They faced the latest Soviet equipment, some of which had been driven directly from tank transports into battle. As noted, Eytan's cunning and the static Arab battle plan resulted in a successful Israeli holding action.

Because of his prowess with delaying tactics in the northern Golan sector, and the shorter distance to Shoham's beleaguered Barak brigade in the south, Eytan used his reserves there. In the southern sector Colonel Shoham had regrouped his survivors that first Saturday night and was now facing another daylight assault. Eytan tried to minimize pressure on the Barak brigade by concentrating his air support against the overwhelming Syrian formations moving relentlessly westward. He set more traps to tempt the Syrians into ambushes sprung by infantry armed with antitank guns.

Israel's holding action was successful. The Israeli forces paid a high price in men and equipment, but they extracted an even higher price from the Syrians. Behind the Syrian front, roads were choked with convoys, which became prime targets. It is estimated that the Arabs went into the Golan battle with a 12 to 1 superiority over the Israeli defenders, and that the loss totals were just the reverse: twelve Syrian tanks lost for each Israeli victim.

RESTRICTING THE SUEZ FOOTHOLD

On the Egyptian front, the holding action did not seem to be fraught with the same imperatives. By 8 October, the Egyptians had managed to move somewhere between seven hundred and eight hundred tanks across the Suez. However, they had little room for maneuver and seemed content to remain in a narrow strip on the eastern bank.

Analysts have questioned why the so-called unified Arab command was apparently not attuned to developments on both fronts. Conduct of the war did not indicate that one ally knew what the other was doing. Such lack of communication allowed the Israelis to determine where they could commit their overtaxed forces without encountering two winner-take-all efforts simultaneously.

Ariel (Arik) Sharon, the second Israeli commander who would add new luster to tank history, operated in the Sinai. But his days of glory in the Yom Kippur War came at the time of counterattack, not during the holding actions.

To head off the original Egyptian advances and buy time, Major General Sharon's tank force headed down the coastal road from Gaza to Port Said on 7 October. Sharon's original assignment was to prevent the Egyptians from fanning out from their bridgeheads into the peninsula.

Sharon was one of the armor heroes of the Six-Day War. After his mandatory retirement he had entered politics. Known as a maverick in his military days, he became an even more controversial figure as he sought elective office. Sharon presented an extreme example of a recalled retired officer who had nothing to lose by disagreeing with the high command, and he never missed an opportunity to do so. Only the excellence of his field performance saved him from a court martial, and then only by a hair.

As Sharon headed toward the northern Egyptian bridgehead, the few remaining Israeli tanks in the Sinai took defensive positions in front of the mountain passes twenty to forty miles from the forward Egyptian tank formations. Military logic suggested that the canal crossing was just the beginning, and that the passes were the next, and main, Arab target. But, perhaps because they were waiting for their missile umbrella to move forward, the Egyptians stayed near the canal. Another reason has been submitted: that the reserve tank forces were being moved across the canal to ensure success in attacking the passes. In any event, it was not until the eighth day of combat that the Egyptians plunged eastward in full force.

HOLDING THE PASSES

The Israeli defenders first spotted huge dust clouds approaching the passes on Saturday, 13 October. A second, and larger, Sinai holding action began the next day, one that dwarfed the battles of the first three days of the war. The number of tanks involved in this battle is unknown, but "reliable sources" indicate that more were engaged than the sixteen hundred British, German, and Italian tanks that fought the Battle of el Alamein, two hundred miles west of Cairo during the same month in 1942.

The Egyptians attacked at dawn, hoping the rising sun would silhouette the defending Israeli tanks. One of the Israeli commanders reported afterward:

> The first wave advanced through a wadi and climbed up onto a plateau to our south. Our forces met them on the plateau, and there was a fierce battle. Within an hour most of the enemy tanks had been wiped out.[7]

The battle remained two-sided, however, with the Israelis suffering heavily with their back to the passes.

The same commander reported that the second Egyptian wave to hit his sector contained a hundred and forty-five tanks:

> When they came into range, I brought up the whole of my forces and we hit them with everything that we had. The Egyptians tried to bring up mobile artillery to support their armor.... [Then] we began hitting their artillery.[8]

The Egyptian commanders knew the odds against success in such an attack. In armored warfare, a rule states that in the absence of surprise, tactical advantage lies with the defense. Heavy numerical superiority is required to compensate. The attackers should have an advantage of no less than 3 to 1 and should be able to isolate enemy contingents. Having watched the week-long Egyptian buildup east of the canal, the Israelis moved some reserve units into the line and reduced the odds to 2 to 1 against them at the time of attack. Superior equipment, training, and position then made the Israelis superior to the Egyptians.

The success of the Israeli holding action in the Sinai terminated the Egyptians' offensive action. The Israelis had not only staved off further advances but also set the stage for the counterattack that would regain the land lost to the Arabs. And the Egyptians had salvaged their national reputation as people who could fight as well as any other nation.

Israeli tank units which were moved into the Sinai holding action that first week of the war were sometimes moving in advance of support services, including medical. A reserve lieutenant colonel, serving with a reconnaissance tank battalion, reported:

> Our tanks picked up casualties and took them along as we advanced because there was no immediate way the men could be evacuated. The Egyptians were fighting well, not running away. Our tactic the first two days was, as usual, to move forward, move forward. But as we advanced, we hit a wall of hundreds of missiles, tanks, and heavy guns. There were heavy casualties on both sides—dead and wounded and burned-out tanks.[9]

On the fourth day, 10 October, the Egyptians attacked by the thousands.

> We let them climb up toward us, and when they were really close we smacked them with everything we had. The next day we captured two Egyptian soldiers. One told us that he had been in the Sinai before the war broke out, preparing an ambush of antitank missiles.[10]

War has its incongruous moments. As dawn lit up the Sinai sky one morning, the commander of an Israeli tank unit counted his vehicles and discovered that he had one too many. An Egyptian armored personnel carrier, lost in the desert night, had attached itself to the column. The Israelis destroyed the vehicle before the Egyptian crew discovered where they were.[11]

CUTTING SUPPLY LINES

Interruption, or interdiction, of supply operations constitutes a major military tactic. Beyond that, when the source of material can be eliminated, supply routes become meaningless. Inasmuch as the major suppliers for the Mideast combatants were the world's two superpowers, no one would attempt to cut off supplies at the source.

The supply activities on both sides were very similar. Except for a few sea shipments, the Soviet supply lines led directly to the heart of Egypt and Syria: huge air transports were landing steadily at Cairo and Damascus. The previous chapter described the aerial highway devised by the United States and the deterrents to potential hostile action. That meant that on both sides, supplies could be stopped only at some point between the rear echelons and the battle zone itself.

The Egyptians' main targets for interdiction were the two north-south roads that Israel had built parallel to the canal. They were part of the multimillion dollar defense network that had been built in this area since the Egyptians had been driven out in 1967. The "Artillery" road, just five miles east of the canal, was designed primarily to range artillery up and down the length of the waterway to repel any invasion attempts. The "Lateral" road, some eighteen miles east of the canal, was to be used for supplying units operating on or near the canal.

From their northern and central bridgeheads, the Egyptian tanks overran the Artillery road in places, but the Israelis destroyed the advance before the lateral supply road fell. Once Israeli reserves were moved into the Sinai action, these roads became important factors in the counteroffensive.

Egypt also tried to disrupt the Israeli east-west supply routes through the mountain passes. Taking advantage of an early moon-set—one of the considerations in selection of the day of attack—helicopters ferried Egyptian commandos on raiding expeditions deep behind Israeli positions, a tactic that was borrowed from the Israeli victory of 1967. Egypt had twenty commando battalions that were considered elite infantry troops. These commando units had been organized by the Egyptian chief of staff, Lt. Gen. Shazli, and he considered them a reflection of his own reputation as a dashing and aggressive combat officer. In any country this brilliant, fiercely devoted soldier would stand out as a talented strategist. Highly respected by his countrymen, he has gained wider recognition as his role in the Arab assault of 1973 has become known.

Shazli represents the typical modern military commander. A graduate of his own country's military academy, he has trained with the armed forces of not one but both superpowers, and he holds a master's degree in political science. He has been a member of the Egyptian officer corps for more than twenty-five years and has been involved in every Israeli-Egyptian conflict.

Part of Shazli's popularity with his men stemmed from his almost mystical belief in the destiny of the Arab people. He is quoted as saying, "Let us regain the glories of Arabism, and prove to the whole world that we are men of war, who either live proudly or die honorably."[12] For Shazli, the commandos were symbols of the revival of Egyptian military capability.

The commandos' fighting ability was offset by the effectiveness of Israeli defensive measures. Several commando-laden helicopters were downed by antiaircraft fire, with total loss of life. One loss was recorded so far south of the main interdiction action that it appeared that the Egyptians intended to move a commando force northward across the Israeli supply lines.

The commando forces deployed in the northern Sinai were surprised to find Israeli units coming at them from the impassable salt-marsh areas that lie along the northern side of the peninsula. The Israeli defenders emerged unexpectedly because they had built in the marsh a floating road capable of supporting men and equipment. These Israeli units were part of the hard-hitting Israeli force that had been sent out to scour the desert, locate Arabs operating behind the lines, and destroy them. Moshe Shoshani was a member of one such unit.

We knew that we were dealing with a fanatical enemy and that no quarter would be taken or given. It was a job for specialists and all of us had been well trained, at one time or another, for this sort of mission. The whole point of the exercise was to hit them hard and absolutely before they had a chance to organize and begin sabotaging our rear lines.

In many ways we were vulnerable to this sort of action. Convoys from the north were moving along narrow arteries and were easy targets for a surprise enemy attack. We knew that the commandos could cause tremendous damage if permitted to plant mines or interfere with our communications networks. This possibility bothered me more than anything else.[13]

In these days of holding actions, while each side was attempting to limit the supplies that the other's fighting force was receiving, the Yom Kippur war of words reached a peak. For example, an Israeli radio broadcast in Arabic beamed west of the Suez proclaimed melodramatically:

> We shall turn your days into nights, and show you the stars at high noon. We shall put your faces and noses in the mud. We shall make the enemy leaders pay heavily for this. We shall crush your bones.[14]

For worldwide consumption, Israel's chief of staff, Lt. Gen. David Elazar, released this statement to the assembled press on the fourth day of the war: "Gentlemen, we have begun the destruction of the Egyptians."[15] That announcement was considerably premature. What the Israeli high command thought would be the start of their counteroffensive became a stunning Egyptian victory. The Sinai campaign became a holding action: the Egyptians would not move from under their missile umbrella, and the Israelis knew that they had to wait for additional reserves and replacement of lost equipment.

In the Egyptian victory, the Israeli 190th Armored Battalion was destroyed. Its commander, Col. Assaf Yagouri, was captured, along with twenty-five tanks. The Egyptians displayed the captured Israeli commander on Cairo television, another phase of the war of words. The Egyptians did not enjoy many such successes once their original thrust lost momentum and the static phase, the holding action, began.

By 14 October, when the Israelis were about to go over to the attack, the two opposing philosophies of battlefield command had begun to play a more significant role in the outcomes of the battles. Egypt insisted on strong central control to the extent that Minister of War General Ismail attempted to run the entire operation from an elaborate underground command post near Cairo. While that technique proved effective in the first days of the attack, Ismail was unable to stay on top of every situation that developed in the open desert. The mobile warfare for which the Israelis had been trained and at which they excelled rendered the rear-area command post less than effective.

Mobile warfare demands a level of initiative among junior officers, a level of confidence in senior ones, and the willingness of both to communicate which the Egyptian Army simply did not possess. The tactic that the Israelis employed on the Golan front was an unplanned, on-the-spot improvisation, an effective reaction of two field commanders faced with a particular type of terrain and overwhelming odds. The search-and-destroy units that roamed the Sinai were able to defeat the Egyptians who were attempting to cut supply lines mainly because of the autonomy of local commanders. They did what had to be done in a given situation and then pulled back to repel the next Egyptian attempt.

Because they would not venture beyond their missile cover and the rigid lines of communication, the Egyptians saw their east-bank holdings between the Second and Third armies being eaten away until they were confined to a narrow belt. With little room to maneuver in the Great Bitter Lake area, they could not adequately defend themselves against counterattack. That point arrived 14 October. In the counterattack phase, General Sharon received his chance.

7

COUNTERATTACK

Most of the factors that had contributed so heavily to early Israeli losses no longer existed by the time the Arab advances had been definitely halted. The element of surprise inherent in a two-front assault by an enemy armed with modern weapons had been removed by sunset on 6 October. The attacking forces of the Yom Kippur War had been found to be better trained, more skillful, and far more courageous than the panic-stricken victims that had fled before the Israelis in 1967.

Some of the new factors played into the hands of the Israeli commanders. Arab strategy became more predictable. Analysis of Russian military doctrine gave clues as to just how the Soviet-trained forces would react. The Israelis could even gauge when the Egyptians would feel that they had consolidated their positions east of the Suez enough to attempt further advances. It also became evident that the Arabs on the two fronts did not have the unified communications that would allow them to exploit their early gains to the fullest advantage. This further strengthened the decision to concentrate countermeasures on the Syrian front while continuing the holding action against the Egyptians.

An evaluation of the situation after the first week of fighting revealed a serious error in Israeli military planning. Because the relatively easy victories of the Six-Day War had been achieved with air power and swift armored conquest of ground positions, little attention had been paid to the development of infantry. They existed, but they had not been honed to the fine degree of sharpness that marked the other service branches. The overwhelming numerical superiority of the Arab armor interlaced with infantry in the Yom Kippur War put Israeli tanks at a distinct disadvantage. The air defense missile umbrella negated Israeli air superiority and covered Arab ground advances against the aircraft. The Israelis then had no choice; they had to work with what they had and attempt to silence the missile sites before they could regain lost ground.

The neutralization of the missiles on the Syrian front was achieved in two ways: Israeli fighters hedgehopped to flanking positions on particular targets before firing and bombing, and the Israelis learned to concentrate their attacks on the computer center that controlled the Syrian air umbrella. When that was neutralized, missile defenses became less effective. Beyond that, the shorter distance to the Syrian capital allowed the Israeli Air Force to launch enough strikes against Damascus so that the Syrians were forced to withdraw missile batteries from the front in order to form a defense ring. Thus the stage was set for the Golan counteroffensive. The war then became the kind at which the Israelis excel: ground forces against ground forces, with unchallenged air superiority.

COUNTERATTACK: GOLAN

The decision to launch the Israeli counteroffensive on the Golan front was not based solely on the logistics involved in getting reserve forces into action on the nearer battlefield. The ever-present international political implications of the Mideast conflict were also important. When it became apparent to the Soviets that the Syrians were not going far beyond their original penetrations, and that Egyptian control of both banks of the Suez made the reopening of that waterway a negotiable reality, it became time to sue for peace.

The early stages of the Russian effort were concentrated in Washington and the United Nations. Knowing that the Americans were anxious to stop the war in any reasonable way, feelers were put out to the state department and to the UN delegation to join in ending the hostilities.

Acceptance of any form of status quo was never considered by the Israeli command. Israel might be able to tolerate the Egyptian presence on the edge of the Sinai, but the Syrians had to be dislodged from the strategic Golan Heights. The urgency of the situation stemmed from the fact that the Russians might decide to replace all of the lost Syrian equipment if the peace overtures were ignored. The counterattack had to be launched before this possibility became a reality. The rugged terrain and concentrated fighting in that area had also been particularly costly to the Israelis in men and equipment. The Syrians had paid even more dearly.

The Syrian commander-in-chief, Maj. Gen. Youssef Chakour, committed two major errors in his initial offensive. Both contributed to eventual failure. First, Chakour had committed too much of the available armor too soon in unfavorable territory with insufficient support. Second, he committed his reserves too fast and did not have sufficient forces available to meet the inevitable Israeli counterattack. The Syrians left behind almost 1,000 of the 1,250 tanks committed; this lost armor was either captured or destroyed.[1]

The Israeli counterattack was orchestrated, to a large degree, by Chaim Bar-Lev, the former chief of staff for whom the Sinai defenses were named. He had retired from the military and was serving as minister of trade and industry. For all of his public bravado, Defense Minister Moshe Dayan sang a different tune privately to Prime Minister Golda Meir. This prompted her to recall Bar-Lev to active duty.

A story has been told of Dayan. Reportedly, he had come to her after visiting the northern and southern fronts and said:

> Golda, I was wrong in everything. We are heading toward a catastrophe. We shall have to withdraw on the Golan Heights to the edge of the escarpment overlooking the valley and in the south in the Sinai passes and hold to the last bullet.[2]

The prime minister wanted a less dramatic, more realistic appraisal. Bar-Lev, reporting on the second day of the war, accepted command on the condition that the assignment be approved by Dayan and the current chief of staff, Lt. Gen. David Elazar.

The latter two not only approved the prime minister's selection, they expanded Bar-Lev's role beyond that of consultant. He was empowered to make command decisions on the spot, and all field commanders were to obey those decisions. In his quiet way, he set about mounting the Israeli counterattack.

Bar-Lev agreed that the Syrian front offered the best conditions for a successful counteroffensive. When he visited the battleground, he found the Israelis had succeeded fairly well in blunting the Syrian advance. The situation, while serious, was manageable.

The entire northern sector was under the command of Maj. Gen. Yizhak Hoffi. The first thing Bar-Lev did was review all standing orders, including Hoffi's. Bar-Lev generally approved the orders' contents, but he emphasized the importance of strengthening antitank obstacles along the main routes to the greatest possible degree. Much of this early contact was with Brig. Gen. Moshe (Mussa) Peled (not related to the commanding general of the Israeli Air Force), who commanded a division in what Bar-Lev perceived to be a critical area for counterattack.

When Bar-Lev returned to Mrs. Meir's office the evening of 7 October, he reported that the ratio of forces was dangerous but not hopeless. They now had three divisions—Peled's, Laner's and Raful Eytan's. The counterattack could begin with a fresh division the following morning. It has been reported that the seventy-five-year-old prime minister looked relieved; she held her right arm up, moving her hand back and forth and saying, "The great Moshe Dayan! One day like this. One day like that!"[3]

With the advantages of an attacking force, the Israelis now began to control the Golan conflict. The decision was made to consolidate positions on Peled's southern flank and to launch the counterattack in his northern sector. This would move his forces northeast toward the center of the front, a decision based on a number of factors. Throughout the holding action and brief stalemate that followed, the Israelis had probed the Syrian lines and felt that they had identified the weakest spots. The northern sector also included flatter terrain that would allow the mass of reserves to exploit any breakthrough. Flat terrain also made enemy tank columns more vulnerable to air attacks.

DAMASCUS EXPRESS

On Monday, 8 October, the counterattack began. The next two days brought repeated acts of individual heroism, continued fierce Syrian opposition, and the loss of several high-ranking Israeli officers. The Israeli fighting mentality again paid dividends in these erratic hours. A second-in-command would quickly replace a lost leader and continue to make the types of decisions that have been the hallmark of Israeli commanders in adapting to conventional situations.

In one instance, reports were received that an enemy tank company was moving around in the rear of Colonel Yossi Peled's brigade and threatening the supply columns. The second-in-command of one of the brigade's battalions, traveling with two half-tracks, had driven over a fold in the ground and suddenly come on six Syrian tanks. As he saw them, this officer instinctively ordered the two half-tracks to charge with all weapons firing. Surprised, the Syrian crews jumped out of their tanks and began to defend themselves with grenades and machine guns. They were wiped out.[4]

The disorganized and haphazard manner in which the Israeli forces had been thrown into battle was highlighted by the fact that the counteroffensive was two days old before Peled could gather his subordinate commanders together to assess the situation and plan ahead.

On the first day of the Golan counterattack, Chakour committed the last of the Syrian reserves, including armor. Chakour, shaken by the death of Syria's best field commander, Brigadier Abrash, put out a call for Arab reinforcements. In response, Iraqis, Moroccans, and Jordanians began to appear on the Syrian front, and Algerians and Kuwaitis on the Egyptian front. Tunisia, Libya, Algeria, the Sudan, and Saudi Arabia also sent token forces to Syria.

Actually, except for an Iraqi reinforced division and three brigades, one from Morocco and two from Jordan, all of the Arab allied reinforcements were token. The liaison between the various Arab forces was poor, if not absent. At one point, the Jordanian Ninety-second Armored Brigade was shelled by Syrian artillery that was itself under attack from Iraqi fighters!

While the opening Israeli thrusts were taking their toll, the Syrian call for reinforcement accentuated the necessity for making a substantial breakthrough before those forces arrived. More important, the Russians decided to replace all of the destroyed equipment. Indeed, the fifth day of the war was nearly as critical as the opening hours. The Israelis simply could not survive a long-term slugging match with a well-equipped enemy. Thus the decision was made to commit all available reserves and fight as though the Golan were the only battle.

With fresh forces available, an attack was launched, with Khusniye and Kuneitra as the objectives. All these attacks were aimed at dislodging the Syrians and threatening Damascus. In the words of Moshe Dayan, "We have to teach the Syrians that the same road that leads from Damascus to Tel Aviv also leads from Tel Aviv to Damascus."[5]

As General Peled's forces advanced toward Kuneitra, they were linking up with Israeli fortifications that had been cut off by the Syrians' original attack. For Peled and his commanders, the meetings with those troops, who had held on under the most trying odds, were an experience they would never forget. The confidence and quiet heroism of the youthful survivors—bloody, dust-covered, and dazed as they were—made the tank crews very humble.[6] The objective was taken, but the real Syrian defeat had yet to be accomplished.

The battle for Khusniye was the hardest. Here, as throughout the fighting retreat across Golan, the Syrians used antitank missiles in approximately the same profusion and effectiveness that marked the early Egyptian battles in the Sinai. The low rock walls of the abandoned fields on the Golan provided excellent cover for Arab defenders armed with RPG-7s. Dug into the fortified rubble of Khusniye, armed with such weapons, the Syrians seemed impregnable. In the end, however, the Israelis appeared to have simply overrun Khusniye.

By contrast, the battle for Kuneitra was over in an hour. After a characteristically heavy preliminary artillery barrage, Israeli tanks charged up the main road and into what had once been the center of town to fight it out at close range. Here again, they relieved a garrison that had been surrounded since the first night of the war. The Syrians had fallen back, leaving a few prisoners behind. The garrison seemed unruffled. "We never worried when the Syrians came through," a nineteen-year-old Israeli infantry captain, late of Brooklyn, said. "We shot them up as they went through the first time and we shot them up when they came running back."[7]

As Wednesday, 10 October, ended, Israeli armored spearheads and infantry had pierced through Syrian defenses and now faced a decision: How much pressure should be brought to bear on the

Syrian capital, and by what route? The Kuneitra-Damascus road lay ahead, but so did the concentration of Arab forces. By looping southward, they could intersect the main highway to the capital and possibly avoid further casualties.

The question was answered for the Israelis. On Thursday morning, the Syrians counterattacked along the road and tried to land commandos behind the Israeli lines. An Arabic-speaking Israeli had monitored the Syrian radio communications that planned the attack, and it was decided to ambush the helicoptered commandos and encircle the Syrian tanks once they were committed to battle. The Syrian attack was fierce and short-lived, and the losses of both sides added to the wreckage-strewn Golan front.

While the massed armor that fought east of the Suez unquestionably represented one of the great tank battles of history, the loss of Arab equipment on the Golan must rank as one of the most fearsome devastations ever recorded. Israeli intelligence reported that most of the Syrian losses were T-54– and T-55–type Russian tanks. But there were also some of the newer T-62 models, many of them seized intact by the Israelis. "For every Syrian tank that had been hit, we found two that were deserted," said General Eytan.[8]

Arab crews had little or no confidence in the survivability of their Russian-supplied armor and were quick to abandon them if hit, or if the likelihood of being hit existed. The small size of the T-54/55/62 has been achieved at the cost of poor internal stowage arrangements and cramped accessibility for the crew. The main fuel tank is located in the forward section on the right side of the crew compartment, with the driver seated to the left. Not only is the fuel tank vulnerable to destruction by penetration of the frontal armor, but the heat generated by the friction of a projectile glancing off the glacis can ignite the fuel without penetrating the armor. This liability to burn from a glancing hit caused observers during the Yom Kippur War to label the Russian tank a "flaming coffin."

THE ARAB LEGION

The Iraqi Third Armored Division of three brigades commanded by General Lafta arrived in Syria and was moved by General Chakour to the southern flank. From there, it attempted an advance on

12 October. Jordan entered the war on Saturday, 13 October, and her Fortieth Armored Brigade, led by Brig. Haled Hajhoui, began to move northward toward Sheikh Miskin. By 15 October, an Israeli task force moved into Saasa, but it was beaten back the next day by a Syrian counterattack and the threat of being struck in the flank by General Safrani's Moroccan troops on the lower ridges of Mount Hermon. By Tuesday, 16 October, the Iraqi Third Armored Division and some Saudi Arabian troops took positions around Kafr Nasij, with the Jordanians at Jasim. The Israelis caught the Arabs, still moving into position, in a dawn ambush, reportedly destroying several tanks during ninety minutes of artillery and air strikes.[9] Nonetheless, the Saasa line held.

Conspicuously absent in the roster of the Arab forces was Israel's Mediterranean neighbor to the immediate north, Lebanon. Convinced that Israel had long been looking for an excuse to annex the fertile region of southern Lebanon below the Litani River, Beirut was anxious to maintain the role of noncombatant. But the situation was not made easier by the Palestinian guerrillas who swarmed into the area along the Lebanese border and fired a number of small rockets at Israeli villages. Though Israel did not immediately retaliate, Lebanon did not emerge from the first week of fighting unscathed. Israeli planes destroyed a radar station on Mount Lebanon, claiming that it was providing information to Syria.[10]

After several days, the Israelis finally slugged their way within artillery range of Damascus and were approaching the Ammon-Damascus Road, settled into the best defensive positions they could find and stopped moving forward.

A combination of reasons seemed to make delay advisable. First and foremost, Israel had received clear signs from the Soviet Union that Damascus must remain off limits. Cutting the Ammon-Damascus Road would have also put Jordan's King Hussein in the position of having to make a greater commitment than the token forces he had already sent. The Israelis were content that there had been no activity on the border between the two countries. Then there was the matter of Israel's slow advance, which had given Syria renewed confidence and a chance to catch its breath. Damascus might be reached, but now only at an unacceptable cost.[11]

For the remainder of the war, this front remained static. The combined Arab armies did launch a series of counterattacks that gained small amounts of territory. An Iraqi-Jordanian force launched an attack against the flank of the Israeli salient with little gain. General Chakour then prepared a joint counterattack, scheduled for 20 October, with two Iraqi armored divisions, an armored brigade from Jordan, and two Syrian armored brigades. However, delays moved the date back to the 23rd; on the 22nd, the cease-fire accepted by Egypt halted action on this front.[12]

Just before the final cease-fire, the Israelis mounted a large-scale attack, including the helicoptering of commandos behind the lines against the Syrian positions on Mount Hermon. The mountaintop positions were taken, but with substantial Israeli losses. This proved to be one of the most expensive operations of the war.

TO THE SOUTH

Understandable confusion exists regarding Israeli actions in the Sinai between what could be called the holding action against the Egyptians and the full-scale counterattack that brought the war to a close. During the first three days, from 6 October to 9 October, the outnumbered Israelis did not engage in classic defensive warfare. They charged past Egyptian advanced positions and appeared at times as though they were going to carry the fighting to the African side of the canal.

Justifying such forays was the existence of the Bar-Lev fortifications. Egyptian assault had overrun these positions and cut off their occupants. It took some time for the field commanders to convince General Headquarters that the men in these bunkers were not contributing to stemming the Egyptian advance and should be withdrawn so they could fight effectively. Israeli tank forces lost much of the freedom of movement needed to cut into and damage the advancing Egyptians by having to move to predetermined positions to coordinate firepower with the fortifications. The Egyptians knew where to expect them and either set ambushes or concentrated devastating firepower against these small harassing forces.

Another confusing element arose out of the difficulty involved in obtaining a clear definition as to when, exactly, the counterattack began, an element that stems from confusion within the Israeli high command. General Sharon had strongly suggested an immediate counterattack as the type of warfare for which the Israelis were best trained. He wanted the assault to take place both on the Golan front and in the Sinai. Some General Headquarters members agreed with him. The books and reports that have been written about the Yom Kippur War do not give Sharon's total view of the conflict, but they contain enough of his statements and actions to indicate that he considered the first Israeli sorties as part of a counterattack.

Because Sharon became such a central figure in the eventual success against the Egyptians, it is well to discuss his position relative to the other commanders at that time.

Sharon had retired from the army as commanding general of the southern command (Sinai) the previous July. He indicated that he resigned from the army because it had been made clear to him that he would not be the next chief of staff.

Sharon represents a strange mixture of characteristics. A born leader of men, he had a natural instinct for sizing up any situation in the most difficult circumstances, not by means of logical processes like staff work but by healthy intuition. By the same token, he was considered a poor staff officer.[13]

Sharon stands as the antithesis of the man who replaced him, Maj. Gen. Shmuel (Gorodish) Gonen. The latter had come to Israel from Lithuania as a child and had risen through the ranks to command the first tank unit to reach the Suez Canal in the battles of 1956. He had then gone to Britain to train at Camberley Staff College in the use of tanks; in 1967, he showed brilliance as he commanded the crack Seventh Armored Brigade in the Sinai. Physically slight, intensely religious, and slightly fussy—he hated his officers to smoke, for instance—Gonen was personally brave and technically competent.[14]

The relations between the two men were further complicated by the fact that Gonen had commanded a reserve division under Sharon. Now, suddenly, the tables were turned; the "junior officer" was in command of General Sharon, who in turn had been given command of Gonen's reserve division. Gonen, taking under his southern command an officer who had been his superior a few months earlier—and one whom every senior, tried, and seasoned officer found extremely difficult to control—set about immediately to do away with the lackadaisical atmosphere and to install more rigid military procedures.

The differences between the two men were never more evident than in their first meeting on the second night of the war. Sharon's reserve division had been held at Tasa, and he helicoptered to Gonen's headquarters Sunday night. He totally disagreed with Gonen's conduct of the war and was positively rude in expressing his opinions. "We were being made to dance to the Egyptian tune," Sharon said afterward, "and nothing was being done to change the tune."[15]

This was an unfair statement. The original failure of Israeli intelligence to anticipate the scope of the Egyptian attack left Gonen with an understrength command; his performance to date could not be questioned. Not only had Gonen's positions been undermanned at the outset, but the decision to win on the Golan front had denied him reinforcements and air support that were being concentrated in the north.

Even the international press seemed to side with Sharon while blaming Gonen for the early Sinai losses. It did appear that the southern commander had lost the respect of his division leaders—led by Sharon. The chief of staff, Elazar, and the war minister, Dayan, spent all Monday night trying to patch up relations between two factions, leaving with the understanding that the Sinai forces were to remain on the defensive until the Syrians were beaten.

SHARON'S COUNTEROFFENSIVE

Against this background, according to an official complaint subsequently filed by Gonen, Sharon launched an attack on Tuesday—against orders. Sharon's version was that Gonen's headquarters did not know what was happening in the field, lost an opportunity to reach the canal, and failed to back up his assault for personal reasons.

Sharon's orders were to relieve a couple of the more desperate outposts on the still beleaguered Bar-Lev Line. The attack was spearheaded by the 190th Armored Battalion. There are confusing reports as to whether this force was carrying out its mission or attempting to lead a counteroffensive back across the canal. In any event, everything went wrong.

The Israelis launched the attack at 1400 hours, 9 October, moving through the undulating sand dunes under heavy artillery fire.

Within fifteen minutes they began receiving antitank fire. The lead group reported that two tanks had been knocked out and the second-in-command killed. Concentrated rocket fire blocked their advance, and they could not see more than one yard ahead because of the black smoke and dust covering the area. The 190th was wiped out, with only two tanks able to retreat from the inferno.

Brig. Hasan Abu Saada, the commander of the defending Egyptian brigade, gave his version of what happened:

> The enemy opened his attack moving forward at a speed of 40 kilometers an hour. As soon as the Israeli tanks crossed the camouflaged infantry trenches, the infantry jumped out of the trenches like devils and began to attack the 190th Brigade [sic]. Our tanks and all the antitank equipment concentrated in the area operated against the enemy and destroyed him. In three minutes, the 190th Armored Brigade [sic] was destroyed.... Assaf Yagouri, the commander, with four other soldiers, was taken prisoner.[16]

Gonen sent what air support he had, but he was unable to push in armor reinforcements. He simply had none to spare. Sharon saw it as failure to support him in trying to expand his already abortive rescue attempt into a canal crossing.

Sharon was so furious with Gonen's lack of support that first Elazar and then Dayan had to intervene. To Elazar, Sharon raged, "Has everyone gone mad? I am certain I can do it. All I need is forty-eight hours to destroy the enemy." "This would be the way to throw the Egyptians off balance," he told Dayan.[17] But Dayan pointed out Israel's desperate shortage of armor in Sinai while the Golan battle sapped its resources. Dayan told Sharon, "You might succeed; but if you fail there is nothing left in Sinai. And the state would be endangered."[18]

The realities of the situation began to be reflected in the Israeli press releases. Earlier, General Elazar had told the press that Israel had begun the destruction of the Egyptian Army. He was replaced as spokesman by Maj. Gen. Aharon Yariv, who warned: "The people of Israel can expect no easy or elegant victories."[19] A review of the exaggerated claims made by the Israelis in the early hours of the conflict caused some veteran newsmen to reflect that the major differences between 1967 and 1973 were that the Israelis had learned to lie like the Arabs, while the Arabs had learned to fight like the Israelis.

The command situation continued to worsen, to the point where Gonen called the chief of staff and asked that Sharon be relieved of his command. It became a matter for discussion at the cabinet meeting on Tuesday evening, 9 October. General Elazar reviewed the Sinai situation with Bar-Lev. They both felt that the counterattack against Syria was going well and that completing the task on the northern front should take first priority. The policy on the Egyptian front should be to endeavor to improve the ratio of forces by allowing the Egyptians to attack and incur casualties against the Israeli defenses. After breaking the major Egyptian attack that had to come, the possibility of counterattacks, including the crossing of the canal, would become feasible.

More important, Bar-Lev was asked to replace Gonen as the general officer in charge in the southern command. Elazar did not think that Gonen had failed in his command but he did feel that the situation that had developed was unhealthy. Bar-Lev accepted on the conditions that a satisfactory arrangement could be made with Gonen, and that the prime minister and the minister of defense should agree. Mrs. Meir called him while he was home packing and thanked him for accepting the post, and Dayan phoned him to say, "Get down there and make decisions."[20]

It was not that easy with Gonen. He felt that he was being dismissed in disgrace while being held responsible for all of the Israeli mistakes in the Sinai. Bar-Lev felt that the command-adviser role he had played in the Golan would not work under the volcanic conditions that existed in the southern command. A compromise was worked out when it was decided to name Bar-Lev as the personal representative of the chief of staff, empowered to speak for him in a command capacity and not as an adviser. To camouflage this move, five other retired generals were recalled and attached to Elazar's staff as advisers.

It was a delicate situation. The compact nature of Israel's ruling class caused its leaders to move back and forth between military command and political office as the situation dictated. This condition had brought political foes together in command positions where such differences should have been put aside. As might be expected, such was not always the case. Sharon saw Bar-Lev's appointment as a political act. He challenged his new leader by shouting at him, "Bar-Lev, since you arrived, you've been thinking only about elections."[21]

That was the first time that Bar-Lev would ask that Sharon be relieved of his command, and each time he would be refused.

COMMAND CONFLICT WEST OF THE CANAL

While the Sharon/Gonen/Bar-Lev arguments were taking place, a strong difference of opinion existed in the Egyptian command regarding the conduct of the war. Ironically, the dissident voice calling for more aggressive action came from an old foe of Sharon: the Egyptian chief of staff, Lt. Gen. Saad el Shazli.

Sharon and Shazli had faced one another in 1967. Shazli came out of the encounter as one of the few Egyptian commanders who was not shamed. Shazli's forces had been surrounded in the eastern Sinai, and Sharon's assignment had been to cut off his retreat. Shazli was able to outmaneuver Sharon to bring his entire division back over the canal in good order.

The argument on the Egyptian side centered on the choice between acting conventionally or adventurously. The conventional tactics were those favored by the commander-in-chief, Gen. Ahmed Ismail; they required his centralized control from the specially constructed underground war room just outside of Cairo. Such tactics also reflected the doctrine of Soviet warfare, that of staging a "meatgrinder" operation against the enemy rather than a blitzkrieg.

The Egyptian moves became more predictable, partly because the conventional approach was also typical of Ismail. For all of the ferociousness of the opening assault, subsequent developments would show that the commander had kept nearly half of his armor west of the canal. The goal became clear: not to plunge across and enlarge the original bridgeheads, nor to carry the war deeper into the Sinai, but to operate defensively to stop any invasion short of Cairo.

Though the first Egyptian use of commandos to cut Israeli lines near the mountain passes had been both premature and costly, Shazli wanted to repeat that tactic with larger forces. Believing that the timing was right, Shazli saw such a tactic as a diversion. His main force would swing around the Israelis from the north and trap them against the canal. As in Sharon's case, there were people in headquarters who supported Shazli's plan.

Ismail claimed afterwards that it was not just a difference in military strategic thinking that caused him to veto Shazli. He felt, probably correctly, that he was more attuned to the president's feeling about the objectives of the conflict and that retaking the entire Sinai had never been considered necessary.

In retrospect, Ismail may have had a more realistic understanding of the officers of the Egyptian Army. While Shazli had unwavering faith in the successful outcome of any undertaking he guided, Ismail recognized that the plan required men with experience in the swift deployment of large formations and ability to make command decisions on the spot. This was neither the background nor the inclination of the average Egyptian officer in 1973.

Much has been made of Ismail's reluctance to move ground forces far beyond the missile umbrella. There is speculation that before the war was a week old, that umbrella was not as strong as it should have been. Some installations had fallen victim to Israeli attacks, but ammunition was also running short. Too many rounds had been wasted in the first few days of fighting.

Thus the conservative approach determined military actions on both sides of the conflict in the Sinai. Not all military strategists agreed with the decisions either at the time or in retrospect, but Israel's Bar-Lev and Egypt's Ismail held the command positions to make their opinions prevail. It probably would not have changed the eventual outcome of the war, but its character would have been different if Sharon and Shazli had had their way.

The war might even have ended with Arab forces heading up the Mediterranean coast and through the passes toward the heartland of Israel, and with Israelis on the road to Cairo. Such a random estimate, of course, disregards the logistics involved in maintaining supply lines to sustain either force.

The Israelis continued the holding action through the first seven days of the war. They also tried to limit the Egyptian build-up east of the canal, without further offensives before the Golan conflict was resolved, at which time they would be ready to counterattack in earnest.

8

FLANKING ATTACK

The attack phase ended. The fighting interregnum between attack and the counterattack passed, in intense localized activity. The stage in the Sinai appeared to be set for an Israeli counterattack. At this point, the two armies sat probing, seeking advantages to exploit, building their forces. On the Israeli side, the personality problems that had plagued command-staff relations had at least been papered over.

To the eventual dismay of the hardworking Egyptians, the situation on the western side of the Sinai front had clarified more than had the situation on the eastern side. Ismail had won out: the war would not be a blitzkrieg but a slow, methodical advance. The Second Egyptian Army would cautiously leapfrog units forward on the central-north sector, while the Third Army would do the same on the southern front.

Caution would dictate every move. The "meat-grinder" advance would, over the long haul, leave fewer Israelis to offer resistance.

In a sense, the Egyptian plan had merit. Israel could not tolerate a meat-grinder war. Cunning, imagination, daring, and ability to take risks would have to characterize the Israeli effort if Israel were to win.

Once Bar-Lev had assumed control in the southern Sinai, the voices urging an imaginative policy began to be heard. Sharon, of course, played first voice in this symphony. He had already received tentative approval, on 12 October, in an orders meeting, for the flanking attack that would, he vowed, "make the Egyptians change their tune and throw them off balance."[1]

On 15 October, Israel launched "Operation Gazelle," the flanking attack that had crossing the Suez Canal as its main objective. But before the fateful battle was joined, the rival armies fought what unquestionably made 14 October the turning point of the Yom Kippur War. In this battle, some two thousand tanks struggled along a line stretching the entire length of the Sinai front. Moving into combat at 0500 hours on a day oppressive with dust, heat, and smoke, the attacking Egyptians failed to take any significant ground, and suffered irreplaceable losses: 110 tanks of the Egyptian Twenty-first Division destroyed on the central front, most of the Third Armored Brigade of the Egyptian Fourth Armored Division wiped out in an effort to breach the Mitla Pass—a total of 264 blasted Egyptian tanks counted in various sectors.

At the report of this Sunday defeat, the Egyptian Second Army commander, Gen. Saad Mamoun, was reportedly stricken with a heart attack. The Egyptian command replaced him with Gen. Abdul Munem Khalil. General Shazli was later reported as assessing the 14 October debacle in strong terms. Egyptian prisoners indicated that Shazli credited the Israelis with outstanding planning and the Israeli SS-11 antitank guided missile as playing a key role in the several engagements that made up the battle.

Despite the setbacks, Egypt's leaders remained confident. The *New York Times* would report on Tuesday, 16 October:

> More recently, with Egyptian positions in the Sinai stabilized, Egyptian diplomats are understood to have been saying to the Europeans in effect that Egypt is still not in any way pressing for a ceasefire, but is listening to what the Europeans say and what they hear from the other side.[2]

For the Israelis, 14 October held fateful promise. The army command issued orders: The canal crossing was to take place the following night. The 14th of October appeared to mark a psychological turning point in the war. Egypt had lost the initiative.

THE PLAN

In the Sinai, the Israelis had been suffering because they had violated a Napoleonic precept specifying unity of command as an absolute

necessity.³ The Sharon-Gonen contretemps had been resolved, however, with the arrival of Bar-Lev—resolved insofar as it could be
without reassignment or removal of one of the participants.

Now Sharon had his way. What has been described as the single,
spectacular tactical coup of the war got under way.⁴

Sharon had little enough to work with: his own division of three
brigades, plus a brigade of paratroopers reinforced by tanks. Adan's
division was to follow Sharon's across the Suez Canal, and a third
division, commanded by Magen, lay ready to cross on order. In the
shadow of the assault units, which included about two hundred
tanks, lay a special force of engineers with earth-moving and other
equipment, including bridging gear. Self-propelled barges had been
brought forward to ferry tanks across the Suez.

Speed was imperative if the entire operation was not to end in
confusion and disaster. Sharon was to drive almost due south from
the area west of the Ismailia Pass. Swinging west, his forces then
had the task of finding a gap, located by Israeli intelligence, between
the Egyptian Second and Third armies. In scrub and sand country,
fighting at night, the armored and motorized force was to circle back
north along the eastern shore of the Great Bitter Lake—with the lake
as flank protection on the left—to secure roads and make the crossing.

The plan called further for a crossing at 2300 hours on
15 October, just five hours after the attack started. That schedule
proved unrealistic: the tanks had to move slowly in the dark, covering
less than five miles an hour, and unexpectedly determined Egyptian
resistance at various points also slowed down the attack force.

There is evidence that Sharon, bullheaded but daring to the last,
and perhaps somewhat too willing to take risks, knew he could not
keep to the timetable. As Herzog has noted:

> . . . Sharon and Brig. Tamir examined the situation and
> knew then that they could never meet the timetable ac-
> cording to the operational order. Sharon said that there
> were three possibilities: (1) to postpone the attack until
> the next night; (2) to clear the area to the canal on the
> night of the 15th and to cross only on the 16th in the
> evening; or (3) to carry out the original plan without ref-
> erence to the timetable which had been laid down. . . .

Sharon felt that had he claimed he was incapable of working according to the planned timetable, Bar-Lev would have agreed to postpone the attack by one day.[5]

Predictably, Sharon decided to go ahead with the flanking maneuver without regard to the timetable. He would then feel his way into the situation and make decisions as required.

The stakes could not have been higher. The Israelis had no troops to spare on the Sinai front. The forces mobilized there had gone through exhausting, day-long battles only a day earlier. In the process, they had lost Maj. Gen. Avraham (Albert) Mandler, one of their best field commanders.

Beyond that, the attack plan flew in the face of military wisdom in several days. The assault forces would have to make their breakthrough, widen and hold the gap in the Egyptian front, and accomplish the Suez crossing simultaneously—all at night. They would be dependent on a single supply line. A major counterattack could cut them off.

Despite the fact that the Egyptian forces in the area of the Chinese Farm, north and east of the canal's point of entry into the Great Bitter Lake, had been depleted and disorganized in the battles of 14 October, they still had great strength east of the canal: two entire armies in addition to missile and other special units. Most importantly, the Egyptian Twenty-first Armored Division sat astride both roads Sharon would have to control to reach the canal. The Egyptian Sixteenth Infantry Division was encamped just to the north.

An important element in any military plan is the accurate delineation of boundary lines between units. These lines keep friendly troops from crossing into each other's zone of fire and indicate areas of responsibility for each commander when attacked. It is important that any prominent geographical feature, such as a road, a village, a hill, or a lake that lies near the boundary line, be wholly inclusive to one or the other linking units, not divided between the two. Otherwise each unit commander will assume that the other is making arrangements for its security.

The boundary line was drawn "through" the Great Bitter Lake, with neither the Second nor Third army made wholly responsible for the lake—a fundamental error that cost the Egyptians dearly.

Yet, the 25-kilometer gap between the Egyptian armies did exist.

The two Egyptian forces, perhaps confident that the lake behind them made a worthless target and thus gave assurance that no attack could be aimed in that direction, lay apart.

The Israeli plan had a curious aspect deriving from Sharon's earlier service in the Sinai. "In the four years he had held Gonen's job, Sharon had studied and even prepared crossing points along the Canal."[6] Near the point where two key roads met at the bank of the canal, Sharon had had the thick sand ramparts thinned down. The weakened section had been marked with red bricks.

Sharon and his troops nonetheless faced a formidable task. Before crossing the canal, they had the long flanking maneuver to complete. That maneuver would increase the eighteen-mile distance from Tasa to the Suez by several miles. While the crossing was under way, supply lines would have to be kept clear. The entire crossing area would have to be protected against Egyptian counterattack. As Sharon said: "The problem was how to reach the water and establish the bridgehead in the same night. We had to do it before daylight, because if we lost surprise, no doubt we would have found quite a number of tanks waiting for us on the other side."[7]

THE ACTUALITY

Out of respect for Egypt's estimated 70,000 troops on the eastern bank, Israeli forces launched a diversionary attack beginning at 1700 hours on 15 October. Colonel Tuvia's brigade attacked almost due west from Tasa, where Sharon had his headquarters. The objective would be Ismailia, on the canal to the west.

The "diversion" had to have all the earmarks of a genuine main effort. Through the late hours of the day and on into the night, Colonel Tuvia's brigade carried the fight to the enemy. Gradually, as the hours passed, the Egyptian Twenty-first Armored Division reacted as had been hoped: the weight of the division's armor shifted north to cover the Tasa-Ismailia road and away from the proposed crossing site. "Right through the night," an Israeli soldier recalled later, "we advanced slowly . . . against fierce resistance."[8]

Tuvia's diversionary attack had been in progress one hour when Sharon moved Colonel Danny Matt's paratroop and Colonel Amnon Reshef's armored brigades to the south. Unobserved in the gathering dusk, these units headed for the gap between General Khalil's Second Army and General Wassel's Third Army. They met no opposition as they approached the Great Bitter Lake and swung back north up the Lexicon road along the lake shore.

Sharon divided this force into three units, each with a key mission. A battalion from Tuvia, attached to Amnon's brigade, moved northwest at the right fork of the junction formed by the Akavish and Lexicon roads, near the top of the lake. The troops of this force were to clear the Akavish road by attacking the rear of Egyptian units guarding it and driving them back toward the Chinese Farm. The farm now lay between this force and Tuvia's brigade which had kicked off to the west at 1700 hours.

Sharon's other two forces had equally sensitive assignments. The Amnon brigade drove north along the Lexicon road branching left from the fork, generally following the canal. The chore, again, was to establish a perimeter around the crossing area. Matt's brigade, aimed straight for the canal, had to cross and clear the way for the parachute and engineer units that would build a bridge and take the ground west of the canal.

Initially, the coordinated attack worked to perfection. The flanking forces turned north as they reached the Lexicon road that ran parallel to the lake; soon afterward, however, the Egyptians came to life. As Amnon Reshef reported, "They woke up and began shooting at the tail of the column from only 40-yard range."[9] Amnon's tanks, forced to deploy to defend themselves, moved into the positions they were to hold during most of the two succeeding days. Both days saw nearly continuous heavy fighting.

The armored battalion heading northeast on the Akavish road also encountered resistance. But it was approaching the Egyptians from behind and had the added advantage of knowing what was happening in a general way. Beyond the Egyptian blocking force, the Israeli paratroopers and engineers of Haim's brigade waited in personnel carriers and buses, unable to move until the road had been cleared.

The linkup took place about midnight. Sharon himself now moved down the Akavish road and by 0130 hours, had crossed the Suez Canal with a command group of about two hundred men.

Token Israeli forces now stood on African soil. Under bright moonlight, in lightly wooded terrain, Sharon savored a peaceful moment. The war seemed far away but for the sound of gunfire from the east bank of the canal.

Moving the heavy bridge and ferry equipment to the canal proceeded while the situation on the eastern bank became more and more fluid. By first light, the Israeli efforts to secure their gains had undergone some adjustments.

SECURING THE 'GAINS

The remainder of that night of 15 and 16 October produced major "if's" for commanders on both sides. Egypt's military leaders could ask themselves whether they might not have destroyed several scattered Israeli armored brigades by taking more decisive action. That question was asked not only in Cairo but elsewhere, particularly after the war had ended. Because of the outcome, the retrospective look on the Egyptian side was extremely searching. Miscalculation, in this instance, appeared to border on the foolish.

> The Egyptian reaction to the Israeli crossing was one of incredulity and light-hearted dismissal, with the various levels of command so blinded by self-adulation at their initial success that they tended to brush the operation off as a tiresome nuisance which could be dealt with. In any case, they argued, it was designed by the Israelis to boost morale in Israel and, as President Sadat put it, to be a spectacular "television operation"—no more.[10]

Israel's top command, for its part, could question the judgment that placed up to seven brigades under maximum risk on a night that saw an impossible battle timetable discarded almost before it had been launched. The timetable called for a canal crossing at 2300 hours and for construction of a bridge and the start of tank-ferrying across the canal before dawn.

None of these things happened on time. At dawn, the irrepressible Sharon was isolated on the west bank of the Suez with his tiny force, effectively separated from his command. In the meantime,

- Amnon brigade had cleared the road near Tirtur and the

Chinese Farm, but Egyptian units that had been bypassed waited until after he passed and closed the road again.

• Heavy resistance in the areas of Tirtur and "Missouri," the dominating high ground on the north side of the Chinese Farm, threatened the main Israeli route to the canal. The corridor came under increasingly heavy fire, and shortly thereafter the prefabricated bridge that was to be thrown across the Suez had become stuck: a section of it had been broken, and Israeli engineers were predicting that repairs would take hours.

Amnon's brigade, trying valiantly to carry out orders, ground into the administrative areas of two Egyptian divisions. The Egyptians began to fire "in all directions, and [the] whole area as far as the eye could see seemed to go up in flames."[11]

The road junction area near the north end of the Great Bitter Lake became the scene of one of the most devastating battles of the war. As Egyptian and Israeli forces struggled for control of the roads, an Israeli parachute unit was wiped out. Repeated attacks by Israeli units failed to dislodge the Egyptians.

The night eventually ended, but morning brought little change except that Egyptian gunners, who could now see what they were shooting at, began zeroing in on the canal crossing place. The first two motorized barges carrying tanks received direct hits and sank with their crews. Israeli sappers had already bulldozed a ravine through the canal embankment and were easing more barges into the water. In three hours, from 0600 to 0900, with the battles still under way only a couple of miles to the east, the Israelis had ferried across some thirty tanks and two thousand men.

Through it all, Sharon remained his debonair self. One Israeli soldier, describing Sharon's mood of confidence on the morning of the sixteenth, said he behaved "like the angel Gabriel."[12]

Most crucially, the element of surprise had been lost. The crossing had been effected and clearly held potential for future decisive initiatives, but on the eastern bank consolidation had been less successful. Significantly, on the Akavish road, two armored battalions were still heavily engaged as they pressed the effort to secure the all-important corridor.

The road junction presented a scene of carnage, with ruined tanks, guns, vehicles, and other wreckage littering the dunes. The "armies clashing by night" had left their collective debris where it had been hit, to the point where "the scene was destruction. . . ."[13] As the same writer noted after a tour of the battlefront:

> The position [near the canal crossing point] had been taken by the Egyptians at the start of the war and was retaken by the Israelis Thursday. . . . [a] burned out hulk of an Israeli halftrack clogged the entrance to the U-shaped position. Its nose was pointed east, away from the Canal.[14]

Some consolidation took place during the first daylight hours at the canal. While Amnon's brigade tried yet again to clear the area around the road junctions, this time aided by two additional tank battalions, the canal crossing continued, by barge. By about 0900 hours, the Israeli bridgehead on the west bank had been extended north three miles.

The prefab bridge had not yet reached the canal and would not be in position until 1600 hours on 17 October. The bridge was still undergoing repairs that, as Sharon told Bar-Lev, would probably take all day. Sharon also called for help in opening up the Tirtur-Lexicon crossroads, where so much effort had already been expended. Bar-Lev alerted Adan's division that it might have to join in the battle for the crossroads. Adan had been waiting to cross the canal on the bridge.

HANGING ON

A new difference of opinion developed between Sharon and the southern command. Sharon felt strongly that the advantage accruing from possession of a foothold west of the canal should be exploited, and as rapidly as possible. Adan's division, in this ultra-aggressive view, should be transported across the canal on 16 October, at which point the Israeli bridgehead forces would continue the attack.

Bar-Lev disagreed. Once on 16 October and again the next day, he refused to allow Adan's units to cross and resume the offensive.

Bar-Lev was not showing indecision. He was, rather, attempting to consider the entire situation as it evolved night and day. He saw that the supply route to the canal had not really been secured. And too, the bridge had not yet been thrown across, making crossings a slow, trying, and dangerous challenge at best. "In his view the tanks [on the west bank] would run to a standstill within 24 hours"—out of gas.[15] Lastly, the Egyptians on the eastern bank were continuing their stubborn fight to prevent further Israeli penetration. Events had already demonstrated that the Egyptians could be extremely tenacious and dangerous. Caution appeared well-advised.

Primarily, the Egyptians seemed to lack the capability to make rapid adjustments. Command decisions took unconscionable amounts of time to bring about movement or change; as a complicating factor, reconnaissance seemed inadequate to cope with the kaleidoscopically changing scene. Thus, information went up through channels slowly in small, virtually useless increments. It is said that General Ismail, commanding the Egyptian side of the war, did not even hear of the Israeli crossing of the canal until late in the morning of 16 October. The crossing had begun eleven hours earlier.

Even more unusual, the news that the canal had been breached was not passed to the Egyptian army commanders on the spot until hours after it had started, and so the counterattack was delayed. Some high officers may not even have understood fully what was occurring. "The reports I received," said Ismail later, "indicated that a small batch of amphibious tanks had infiltrated, and it was the conviction of the local command that they would be wiped out quickly."[16]

While pressure on the contested eastern bank of the canal began to concentrate in the area of the Chinese Farm, the west-bank units slowly expanded their bridgehead. They were hanging on rather than blasting ahead, in accordance with the decision already made by Bar-Lev. Egypt still had powerful forces in the area; if the Israeli troops lost control of the roads and blocking positions near the canal bank, the chance for success in the operation would have been wasted.

Sharon would not hold strictly to orders. On his own, he split his small force into raiding parties and turned them loose. They began to search for SAM sites, convoys, fuel dumps, and anything else worth attacking. They did find and destroy four SAM complexes, leaving a huge hole in the Egyptian missile umbrella and opening up the possibility of Israeli air exploitation of the gap.

Sharon remained his bouncy self. One of his aides asked what he would do if the Israeli command took away his commission. "So?" said Sharon. "I'd join up under another name."[17]

In the end, the results appeared to tie together the small insubordinations and inconsistencies. But the men who made the operation work were fighting on the eastern bank, not the western. The experience of Adan and others, junior in rank to Sharon, was more or less typical. As Chaim Herzog wrote:

> While this battle [for the crossroads area] was raging Bren [Adan] ordered two brigades to move and to clear the area of Akavish and Tirtur: Natka's brigade deployed to the south of Akavish, moving northwards . . . and continuing in the direction of Tirtur; Gaby's pushed from east to west. Tuvia's brigade too having come under his command, Bren pressed on the Egyptian forces in the Israeli corridor from east to west with three concentrated armored brigades. Bren's forces evacuated the paratroopers from the field at 11:00 in the morning, but as this battle was developing, a report was received that an Egyptian armored brigade was moving up from the south near Lexicon along the coast of the Bitter Lake. Bren asked for the Karen brigade and received it.[18]

Once again, speed of decision and flexibility decided the issue. In the battle of movement to the south of the crossroads, the Israelis' capability for swift adjustment made the difference: the counterattack mounted by the Egyptian Twenty-fifth Armored Brigade broke down, then dissolved entirely as the surviving crews fled. They had actually entered a trap from which they could not be extricated. Eighty-six of ninety-six tanks in the unit were destroyed.

Chain effects were at work again. Losses suffered by the Egyptians in the counterattack from the south were seen in retrospect to have had a direct influence on the developing battle of the Chinese Farm. The threat from the south, if not eliminated, would have occupied Israeli forces that could not be spared.

After nightfall on 16 October the Egyptians finally launched the coordinated counterattack that had been expected much earlier. Why had it not come sooner? The answer may explain why Sharon's bold move did not end in disaster. As one account put it, oversimplifying but making a key point: "Ultimately, Sharon's bridgehead was saved by a single fact: to mount an operation involving both the Egyptian Second and Third armies, it was necessary to circulate orders bearing signatures from four different staff officers."[19]

9

BREAKTHROUGH AND ENVELOPMENT

The Chinese Farm had been established as an experimental agricultural station under President Nasser. Much of the machinery had been imported from Japan; Israeli soldiers, seeing the Japanese inscriptions and not familiar with Oriental scripts, named the site the Chinese Farm during the 1967 Six-Day War.[1]

The Farm was honeycombed with irrigation ditches that made perfect hiding places for infantry, and Egyptian troops used these to good effect the night of 15 October. But the farm's location just northeast of the network of roads that led to the canal north of the Great Bitter Lake gave the site its particular tactical significance. The army that held the farm could control not only the road junctions but the canal crossing-place as well: the latter fell easily within artillery and rocket range of batteries emplaced on the farm.

The savage fighting at the Chinese Farm seemed to belie later contentions that the Egyptians had not yet fully assessed the meaning of the Israeli flanking maneuver, breakthrough, and canal crossing. Other evidence, however, suggested that that was indeed the case. Egyptian reaction was piecemeal; it even took place at times in illogical fashion. A Moroccan brigade based in Cairo was rushed south to join the Third Army—even though that army, lying south and east of the Great Bitter Lake, stood in mortal danger of being cut off from the rear. That would come with Israeli exploitation of the bridgehead, and such exploitation had already been launched, probingly, on 16 and 17 October.

Lack of appreciation of the situation appeared most flagrantly at the level of Egypt's high officialdom and top army command. President Sadat and General Ismail both attended the jubilant session of the Egyptian Parliament that took place on 16 October. At no time in this session was the Israeli penetration to and crossing of the canal mentioned. Field reports that came in during the remainder of that day stressed that the bridgehead force would soon be liquidated—and, in fact, a force detached by the Second Army did attack Danny Matt's bridgehead units on 17 October. But none of the battlefield action changed the basic fact that the Israeli stroke could basically alter, and possibly end, the war in the Sinai region if not quickly contained.

The political situation was changing while the battlefield action was taking place. The Israeli canal crossing had begun to give the Soviet Union second thoughts about its Arab allies. Soon pressures for an end to the war would increase.

At the Chinese Farm, on the evening of 16 October, none of these concerns mattered much to the local commanders. The issue had been joined; the counterattack had begun.

BATTLE OF THE FARM

Men on both sides had to call on their last reserves of energy as the Chinese Farm battle took its toll. It should be remembered in this connection that fighting in the area had progressed under the most confused circumstances for twenty-four hours. Earlier, units on both sides had been involved in the great armored struggle that took place on 14 October. Simple weariness became a factor.

Bren Adan's division had been picked to join in the canal crossing—and still had that mission. First, however, certain east-bank problems had to be attended to. By the evening of 16 October, Adan had fought his way down to the Chinese Farm. Here he linked up with the Amnon armored brigade.

Amnon Reshef's private war could provide the material for a separate study. He had asked to be the first to cross the canal but instead had been given the task of securing the perimeter. That decision was based on sound reasoning, he knew the area well. By the time the battle for the Chinese Farm had ended, his command "had suffered nearly 100 percent casualties—for the third time since Yom Kippur."[2]

THE MULTIPLE FRONTS

No "front," in the conventional sense, existed at the Chinese Farm. Once again, improvisation became the order of the day. To complicate the situation, the battle was waged initially at night, with attendant disadvantage to both sides. The Egyptian infantryman found it difficult, under these conditions, to make effective use of his anti-tank missiles, while darkness cut down the effectiveness of the Israelis' tank gunnery.

In the confused fighting at the farm, Israeli tanks came under fire from Egyptian units attacking principally from the north. But at no point could they assume that they had secured their flanks and rear. Shells and rockets came at them from two and sometimes three directions.

For the engineers seeking to throw the bridge across the Suez Canal, the Chinese Farm fighting provided an umbrella of sorts. The absolutely Homeric task of moving the 190-yard-long bridge structure, towed by a dozen tanks and moving on rollers, bogged down several times as the Chinese Farm battle progressed.

On the morning of 17 October, the battle was well under way and giving no signs of slackening. With daylight, too, the Israeli forces in the bridgehead came under intense fire for the first time, a factor that augmented the importance of the Chinese Farm effort. Matt's headquarters on the west bank took a hit from an artillery shell, and Matt's deputy was wounded. Fighting actually continued for the next six days until the cease-fire. "As guns, mortars, and Katyushas combined to pour tens of thousands of shells into the area of the crossing."[3]

A new factor emerged on 17 October. Because Sharon had cut a fifteen-mile hold in the Egyptian missile curtain, the Israeli Air Force could again fly in the canal area north of the Great Bitter Lake. Thus the Egyptian planes seeking to wreak maximum damage on the bridgehead themselves came under attack from Israeli planes. Egyptian aircraft losses mounted.

Egyptian helicopters came in on suicide missions to drop barrels of napalm on the bridge and the bridgehead; large numbers were shot down. FROG surface-to-air missiles were employed, but the Israeli forces soon learned how to bring them down with antiaircraft fire.[4]

The Chinese Farm battle had to end, and it did on 18 October. The Amnon brigade, thrown into the battle, finally turned the tide. Reorganized while out of action briefly, the brigade took the Chinese Farm, still held by Egyptian Second Army units, from the rear, or the west side. "The Egyptian forces had by now been worn down by the intense fighting and this time the Israeli attack was successful. The Chinese Farm fell."[5]

Somewhat to the astonishment of the Israeli attackers, the Egyptian defenders of the farm left nearly everything behind as they retreated. The fields, the central feature of an extraordinarily well-organized defensive complex, became littered with war materiel—antitank weapons, Sagger missiles, antitank guns, and much more. Pressing north to follow up the advantage, Amnon's brigade moved a full three miles, expanding the area of Israeli control north of the lake.

On the afternoon of 18 October, Moshe Dayan visited the scene with Sharon and Reshef. The latter has been quoted as terming the field a "valley of death," while Dayan, viewing the flotsam and jetsam of war in amazement, could only murmur, "What you people have done here!"[6] Egyptian forces had lost an estimated hundred tanks on an extraordinarily constricted front.

DEFINING A BATTLE

The difficulty one encounters in separating the Chinese Farm battle from the armor and infantry clashes going on simultaneously in the other sectors springs from the fact that the Chinese Farm struggle grew out of, and in a sense belonged to, both the earlier and later battles. It also belonged to concurrent fighting. When Reshef bypassed the farm the night of 15 October, he was in effect touching off the battle; the Egyptian infantrymen and tankers who popped out of the ditches and began firing at his rear were continuing it. At no time thereafter until the Egyptian evacuation was the farm a scene of peace.

The battle of the Chinese Farm can, however, be identified. Strictly speaking, it began with the Egyptian counterattack the night of 16 October. It included the abortive effort of the Egyptian Twenty-fifth Armored Brigade to move up the lake shore to relieve the defenders of the farm. The battle then ran its course at and around the farm until 18 October.

The ways in which the Israeli and Egyptian commands asked for and received double and triple duty from its personnel at this critical juncture of the war can only arouse admiration. But on the Israeli side, the plans and their modes of execution swept the leadership along; the leaders had to bob with the tide, make adjustments here and there, hold units such as Adan's back pending the outcomes of localized clashes, and in general orchestrate the proceedings and hope for the best. Some of the forces the Israelis had to orchestrate, among them Sharon's command, closely resembled the tiger that was easy to mount and difficult to dismount.

The main difference between the adversaries in the Sinai lay again in the quality of leadership in the field. On both sides, the soldiery fought with dedication and intensity. But Egypt went into Operation Gazelle with a substantial record of success, a considerable amount of territory on the east bank, and invaluable experience in Israeli ways of waging war. Egypt came out of Operation Gazelle with its east-bank command split apart and with Israel in possession of a major bridgehead on the west bank. The Third Army had been all but isolated and was immobilized.

It should be noted that the Chinese Farm battle was so closely related to the Suez Canal crossing as to be a part of that operation. The Egyptians chose the Chinese Farm as the objective of the counterattack because possession of the farm would give the counterattacking forces the capability of interdicting further movement across the canal. As the battle continued, the engineers struggling with their bridges under fire acknowledged the significance of the fighting in simple terms: "They closed the road behind us," said one.[7] Another reported: "Our boys were . . . a target for all the guns and planes in the neighborhood. . . . Everybody here lost a friend."[8]

In the end, the battle of the farm had the effect of reducing the amount of firepower the Egyptians could throw at the crossing point. To the degree that it did so, it saved Sharon's spectacular coup.

One series of circumstances both connected with and unrelated to the battle of the Chinese Farm suggests the truth of the adage that it is better to be lucky than smart. As the counterattack took shape in Egyptian plans, Colonel Shazli, of earlier fame, was asked to head up the forces assigned to contain the Israeli bridgehead. This occurred on 16 October, before the counterattack at the Chinese Farm actually got moving.

An aura of mystery surrounds the events that followed. Certainly Shazli was unable with local forces either to contain or reduce the bridgehead. Sadat later spoke frankly of the command problems the Egyptians had encountered, glossing over only the details of Shazli's activities. In Sadat's words,

> When the Israeli forces made their counterattack on October 16, I ordered General Shazli [then Chief-of-Staff] to go personally to Ismailia within 90 minutes to hold the Israelis within the limits we had already defined around the Lake.
>
> I do not want to go into the details of the events that occurred during the next three days. But on Friday, October 19, the War Minister, General Ahmed Ismail, called me after midnight. I went to the Command Headquarters to find General Shazli collapsed. He was saying that the War was over, a disaster had struck, and that we had to withdraw entirely from Sinai. . . .
>
> I was afraid that Shazli's despair might demoralize the other commanders in the operations room—which was Israel's main purpose of the operation. So I relieved General Shazli and appointed General Adel Ghani el Gamasy in his place.[9]

The "generous" Sadat forgave Shazli his lapse, if lapse there was. "The men had crossed the Canal and stormed the Bar-Lev Line . . . the collapse he suffered later was only human."[10] Shazli did not suffer a collapse, but the Egyptian history of the war would require someone to blame, and Sadat was not going to be that someone. Sadat even kept the fact of Shazli's removal secret for two months after the war was over. Sadat realized that Shazli was, in the eyes of the Egyptian soldier, the Egyptian Army, and an announcement of his removal at that time could trigger uncontrollable events.

CRITICAL FACTOR: TIME

"Enemy territory," noted the instructions on a historical simulation game called *Sinai*, "is defined as hexagons which were enemy-held at the start of the game." The instructions continue:

> Territory can only be captured by units which are in communication with their supply sources. A unit is in communication with its supply source if it is in supply or if it is in a friendly unit (which is in supply) by a continuous line of hexes occupied by friendly units or covered by uncontested Zones of Control. A Zone of Control is contested when it is overlapped by an Enemy Zone of Control or an enemy unit.[11]

The game, despite its dehumanized, computerized style, had meaning and truth for the real-life battlefield. The situation in which a "unit is in communication with its supply source if it is . . . covered by uncontested Zones of Control" had virtually been defined, in reverse, by the case of the Egyptian Third Army by 19 October. As of that date, Sadat asked Premier Kosygin, of the Soviet Union, to call a meeting of the United Nations Security Council and arrange for a cease-fire.

The Egyptian Third Army's lines of communication were being cut. Israeli forces on the west bank of the canal were launching the series of overlapping and mutually reinforcing armored sweeps that would take them to the Gulf of Suez and north to Ismailia. Resistance by the Egyptian Second Army near "Missouri," on the east bank, was slowly being ground down. The Israeli "television operation" that had leapfrogged the canal (the Egyptians too, until about 19 October, were calling the advance an "armored commando raid") had succeeded beyond Sharon's most sanguine dreams, and Israel was running out of time.

Two reasons have been cited for the phenomenon of an army and state that, at the height of a spectacular military comeback, began to feel the pressure of the clock. First, the world's great powers, and in particular the Soviet Union, felt deepening anxiety as they watched the spreading debacle in the Sinai and on the west bank of the Suez Canal. The Soviet Union saw all the early Egyptian accomplishments of the war evaporating, knowing that losers may become laughingstocks when they sue for peace. Still possessing large areas of the Sinai desert, however, the Egyptians might bargain and come out ahead—or at least even. No one would have lost face, meaning, in Soviet terms, international influence and prestige. The Soviet Union definitely did not want another total Arab military collapse.

The second reason had to do with oil. Indirect pressure, in the form of reduced oil shipments to western countries from the Arab states, had been exerted on Israel since the second week of the war. Israel itself seemed relatively secure as regards oil supplies, and this would remain true at least as long as the Abu Rodeis oil fields, on the west coast of the Sinai, remained under Israeli control and the Shah of Iran stayed friendly. Also, the United States in 1973 seemed impervious to such material pressures, and the United States ranked as Israel's one indispensable ally.

Nonetheless, the Arab states made an effort to use oil as a club. As one writer noted:

> The long-awaited formal decision to use oil as a weapon in the "Middle East Conflict" was announced at the end of an eight-hour meeting in Kuwait of ministers from 11 countries. The monthly export reduction was set at 5 percent of each previous month's sale, starting with the level of sales in September. The measure was at once more modest, more flexible and vaguer than had been predicted.[12]

The club had become a switch. But three days later, one country, Saudi Arabia, stopped all oil exports to the United States.

A third reason why time pressed on Israel concerned Arab pride. Essentially, none of the superpowers, including the United States, could stand by and watch a total Arab—or Egyptian—defeat without planting the seeds of the fifth Arab-Israeli war.

Israel's leaders could assess the meaning of these imponderables as well as anyone in Washington, Moscow, or Cairo. But Israeli leaders may not have understood the degree to which the super-powers controlled the dance of death.

The elements of time and timing affected developments on the battlefield as well as those in the state council rooms. As regards timing, Israeli forces continued their controlled rush into Egypt's rear areas. As for time, as late as 21 October, a day on which the U.S. secretary of state, Henry Kissinger, flew to Moscow for "con-sultations" at the urgent invitation of the Soviet leaders, Israeli forces slicing into Africa thought they had plenty of time.

> . . . In Israel there was great skepticism about a cease-fire. In fact few believed that one was imminent. . . . Visiting Sharon's division on 21 October Deputy Prime Minister Yigal Allon assured them that they had ample time and that there was no hurry.[13]

A day later, on 22 October, the United Nations Security Council met at dawn and passed Security Council Resolution 338. The res-olution called for a cease-fire that would start within twelve hours and that would not be delayed beyond 1852 hours on the evening of the same day.

Timing now became less important to the combat forces than time. A sense of urgency spurred the Israeli attack units on. Where relative prudence had governed troops and vehicle movements, and where attack and maneuver had proceeded in accordance with tested principles, a final effort was launched in which caution was thrown to the winds. For the Israelis, the objective now became more simple than the encirclement of the Third Army or the destruction of enemy forces. The game now was to improve the posture of the Israeli armies in the hours remaining so they could go into the cease-fire with the best possible position.

For the Arabs, a similar situation existed, but in reverse. The desperate straits of the Third Army added a dimension and forced the hands of local commanders.

Bren Adan had moved across the canal following the successful termination of the battle of the Chinese Farm. He became instru-mental, as a field commander, in expanding the bridgehead west of the canal. Now he was asked to advance to the area of Lituf, at the point where the Little Bitter Lake joins the Suez Canal.

This occurred on the morning of 22 October. Adan mounted a

pincer attack aimed at clearing the shores of the lake and the roads paralleling it. Aided by two other brigades, and working in coordination with his Natke brigade, Adan's forces began encountering fierce resistance almost at once. The Egyptian Third Army was actually fighting to preserve its road contacts with Cairo—two main routes known as Asor and Sarag. At the urging of Bar-Lev, Adan in the afternoon ceased to press the battle along the more southerly of these roads, Sarag, and concentrated on Asor.

With the cease-fire deadline almost at hand, Adan ordered his three brigades to storm the opposing positions in an effort to reach the lake. These attacks succeeded, and by 1800 hours Adan's troops had charged through the positions along the Little Bitter Lake and reached the canal. Herzog has reported that one of the battalions from the Karen brigade mounted an Egyptian rampart at the south end of the Little Bitter Lake and deployed along it.[14] That night, the battalion was nearly destroyed when it came under heavy Egyptian artillery fire.

In a sense, the cease-fire came too soon. The diplomats for once had outstripped the army commands. As it turned out, the armies could not call off the war so suddenly; the cease-fire was violated on both the Egyptian Third Army and the Syrian fronts. The war continued for two more days as the rival commands desperately tried to establish favorable conditions for postwar negotiations.

Tel Aviv, Damascus, and Cairo had agreed to the cease-fire terms, but agreement could not be made binding on some of the field commanders. Both sides later defended their actions as battlefield alternatives forced on them by the enemy. At least one correspondent, however, saw the Israeli movements in a different light: ". . . the Israelis appeared to be engaged in what is known as 'line straightening' among military men."[15]

On 23 October, the isolation of the Third Army had become complete. From monitored radio conversations, Israeli forces knew that field commanders on the Egyptian side understood what was happening. Segments of one series of such conversations went as follows:

> 19th Brigade Commander of Third Armored Commander: "We emphasize that the [cutting of the Suez City-Cairo road] has cut off all supplies to you. . . ."

19th Brigade Commander to General Kabil a few minutes later: "The Suez Road is cut, Kabil. We have to open
the Suez Road at kilometer 109 where I am locked in and
you are on the outside. I tell you, Kabil, that the army is
being surrounded. It is not in Arab hands. Open the Suez
Road for me. . . ."

General Wassel to General Ismail, still later: "Kabil
refuses absolutely to cooperate with us. . . ."[16]

General Kabil appreciated the dispositions more than most. He
skillfully employed his unit to fight, an elusive delaying action to buy
time for units of the First Army to arrive.

These and similar messages became important later when the
Soviet Union charged that the Third Army had not been cut off at
the time of the 22 October cease-fire. But few would listen. The Soviet claim had the purpose, in part, of placing on the United States
and Israel the responsibility for prolonging a war whose end had
been programmed. Later investigation would strongly suggest that
Israeli forces pursuing their own local goals had been, in a sense,
out of control, to the point where they made America's calls for a
conclusion to the war appear in Soviet eyes as steps to betrayal.

On 24 October, fighting continued as Israeli forces drove on Suez
City. Once there, tank and parachute units began to move into the
city. They came under heavy fire from all sides.

Within minutes twenty of the twenty-four tank commanders of the column . . . were killed or wounded. The
tanks continued their charge forward to the end of the road.
The paratroopers came under fire and when some of their
vehicles were hit, they jumped out and took shelter in the
adjoining houses. This had not been envisaged as a major
operation . . . , but rather as a routine mopping up operation against an enemy who was cut off and disintegrating.
The troops were therefore psychologically unprepared for
such a situation; furthermore, they could not even distin-
guish where the enemy fire was coming from.[17]

Thus, like grappling wrestlers, the armies lay locked in battle,
one action triggering another. Earlier, Egyptian gunners had fired on
Israeli supply columns thundering across the Suez on three bridges,

claiming that this Israeli supply operation on Monday night, 22 October, coming after the first official cease-fire, had constituted "military action" as prohibited by the cease-fire order. As such, ran the argument, the supply movement had forced retaliations. Now, on 24 October, the Israelis had to attempt the rescue of the remnants of two parachute units isolated in Suez City.

In the end, the two units escaped under cover of night. General Gonen personally supervised the operation from outside the city, first conversing by radio with the captain in command; the actual commander, a colonel, lay wounded and semiconscious among the trapped paratroopers. Gonen eventually guided this second and last group of survivors out of the city by radio, street by street. "Suez," one account maintained in a footnote to this terminal battle of the war, "was a grave error costing some 80 killed."[18]

The Suez City fighting nonetheless belongs in the traditions of Israeli arms and, as such, must be considered an extension of the entire bridgehead operation.

> [The Israelis have] the taste for sudden, swift attack, prefaced by extremely thorough technical preparations combined with a perfect secrecy.... The basic forms of war as waged by the Israelis are the ambuscade and, especially, the lightning raid. We find these tactics already in the Bible....[19]

The battle of Suez City ended almost with the end of the war. On 24 October, a second cease-fire was proclaimed. Despite more fighting on the southern front, the second UN order brought the war to a halt, but too late to turn aside the extraordinary series of circumstances that led to a Soviet–United States nuclear confrontation. That confrontation took place on 24 and 25 October. Key moves included a Soviet threat to intervene in the Yom Kippur drama and an American combat alert that positioned U.S. forces around the world in Defense Condition 3, meaning that all American troops across the world were placed on standby, awaiting orders with all leaves cancelled.

The UN resolutions had given Sadat hope that the United States, the Soviet Union, and the United Nations would guarantee an Israeli adherence to the cease-fire and the holding of a peace conference to finally settle this anachronistic dispute. On 24 October, Egypt, with difficulty, persuaded Syria to accept the 22 October cease-fire resolution and not launch a prepared counterattack against the Israeli salient.

News reached Cairo later, however, that UN observers sent to enforce the second cease-fire were stopped by Israeli forces. Sadat fired a message to Brezhnev advising him of the situation and requested Soviet troops to open the Third Army supply road.

Brezhnev and President Nixon were in contact through appointed subordinates, Ambassador Dobrynin and Secretary of State Kissinger. The Soviets suggested that "if the Israelis are not going to adhere to the cease-fire, let us work together to impose the cease-fire, if necessary by force."[20] Nixon, acting on Kissinger's advice, rejected the proposal. Kissinger was later to say, as reported in the *New York Times* of 26 October 1973, that he gave the Israelis an extra four days of fighting time by delaying the conclusion of the Israeli-Egyptian cease-fire.[21]

The Soviet ambassador to the UN, Jakob Malik, spoke for Egypt's request for troops, saying that it was "entirely justified" and adding that the United States was responsible for making Israel observe the cease-fire. Dobrynin then delivered a message to Kissinger near midnight of the 24th, stating, "We strongly urge that both send forces to enforce the cease-fire and, if you do not, we may be obliged to consider action alone."[22]

U.S. intelligence supported the Soviet intention to use force. Transport aircraft used in the Arab resupply airlift were diverted to staging bases of seven airborne divisions in the Soviet Union. Israeli intelligence reasoned that the airborne division would attack Israeli forces on the West Bank, while two Soviet mechanized divisions would attack through Syria, supported by amphibious landings of naval infantry.

The Washington Action Committee of the National Security Council met in the White House War Room. Kissinger and Secretary of Defense James R. Schlesinger convinced Nixon that the United States had to escalate its military posture to avoid giving an impression of weakness. At 12:10 A.M. on 25 October, all commands were put on Defense Condition 3, more commonly referred to as "Red Alert."

Aircraft carriers were moved, marines positioned, army paratroops and air transports readied, and B52s flown in from Guam.

During the next twenty-four hours, the world held its breath. Was this to be the prophesied Battle of Armageddon?

On 26 October, Ambassador Dobrynin "explained" to Kissinger that Brezhnev believed the Americans to be in collusion with the Israelis to ignore the cease-fire in the south sector of the canal zone, and that the fate of the Third Army rested in American hands. Kissinger understood the deeper implications and immediately demanded that Israel open the Third Army's supply road. This they did and tensions lessened, though the U.S. alert was not called off for some days.

A seven-thousand-man UN peace-keeping force, under the command of Finnish Lt. Gen. Ensid Siilasvuo, was put in place between the belligerents, and kilometer 101 became the site of the Egyptian-Israeli cease-fire and disengagement talks.

The threat of a world war had passed.

10

FINAL POSITIONS
AND THE FUTURE

On Israel's northern front, as on the southern, the war had flared once more at the time of the 22 October cease-fire. Israeli commandos of the Golani Brigade were helicoptered to landing zones high up on Mount Hermon where the war had begun less than three weeks earlier. In bitter fighting, Israeli troops wrested the key heights from the Syrian defenders. Both sides took heavy casualties in this battle that began on 21 October and continued through much of the next day.

The battle in the north bore a superficial resemblance to the battle in Suez City. The terrain was different in the two cases, and the two battles had different purposes. On Mount Hermon, Israeli troops sought to regain tactically important ground that Israel had controlled when the war started. In Suez, the Israeli attack was intended to drive a final nail in the coffin of the Egyptian Third Army. But both battles reflected Israeli pride. Israel wanted to be in position on the Golan Heights when the war actually ended if only to be able to say that the original border between Israel and Syria had been restored. Suez City seemed to present a final target for combat units completing a brilliant victory, the final plum to be plucked as the desert campaign came to an end.

As regards military significance, the two objectives, Mount Hermon and Suez City, lay poles apart. Holding the former, Israel had nothing that added materially to the gains already registered.

Significantly, the separate battles had different outcomes.

Where the Syrians were driven from Mount Hermon, completing the recapture of the Golan Heights, "... when the cease-fire took precarious effect on October 25, the devastated ruins of Suez were still in Egyptian hands."[1]

The second cease-fire actually put an end to the war. This armistice took effect at 1700 hours on 24 October, but even then incidents erupted at various points in the air, land, and water battle zones. "An Israeli freighter flying a Liberian flag would be mined in the Gulf of Suez. Furtive Egyptian helicopter commando movements would be detected and the offenders punished with quick bursts of machine-gun fire and air-to-air rockets."[2]

COSTS VERSUS ACQUISITIONS

Israel came out of the Yom Kippur War with several hundred square miles of territory that it had not held prior to 6 October. But the territory alone hardly made the war more than a Pyrrhic victory: it was "territory they [the Israelis] did not need. . . ."[3] In addition, parts of two Egyptian armies still "held" equally sizable blocks of ground east of the Suez Canal.

A study of maps showing the "before" and "after" situations on the northern and southern fronts reveals some interesting facts. On 6 October, the 1967 cease-fire line ran in a rough, elongated half-circle from a point just east of the southern end of the Sea of Galilee to the Lebanese border. Inside that line, on the Israeli side, were Rafid, Khusniye, and Kuneitra. On 25 October, a bulge pointing directly east into Syria had been superimposed on the northern end of the original line. Inside that bulge, which covered perhaps three hundred and fifty square miles, lay, in addition to the towns already named, Jeba and Ahmadiya. The Golan Heights, of course, lay inside the perimeter that had been purchased at the cost of so much blood.

In the south, the Suez Canal and its lakes, Timsah to the north and the Bitter Lakes to the south, had formed the dividing line between Egyptian and Israeli-held territory. The only exception was a triangle of land enclosing Port Faud in the extreme north. On 25 October, the Israelis held an hourglass-shaped piece of Egypt, some nine hundred square miles in extent, that ran from just south of Ismailia to a few miles south of Suez City. The entire west bank of the connecting Bitter Lakes lay well inside the Israeli-held land. Suez City lay inside the perimeter as well, but, as noted, the city itself remained largely in Egyptian hands. Israeli troops had penetrated to within fifty miles of Cairo.

East of the canal, the anomaly appears. The Egyptian Third Army, numbering twenty thousand to thirty thousand troops, occupied the entire east bank of the Little Bitter Lake and the stretch of the eastern shore of the Gulf of Suez. Further north, the Second Army held a long, narrow strip of territory on the east bank, running from just south of Ismailia to the Mediterranean and including Port Faud.

As for losses in men and equipment, the figures tell a frightening story. A total of 2,355 Israeli soldiers had been reported killed; 508 others were missing, including 182 believed dead.[4] The Israelis also suffered approximately nine thousand wounded. Egypt and Syria, the key Arab powers in the war, had lost an estimated fifteen thousand troops, among them five thousand dead.

Tank and aircraft losses add a grim footnote to the balance sheet. The Arabs have been reported as losing 370 planes and the Israelis 115, a total of 485. The total of Arab tanks destroyed on the northern and southern fronts came to 1,274, while the Israelis lost 420. The figures have been described as "less than might have been expected considering the great destructive power of the modern tank compared with its counterpart of three decades before."[5] But the conclusion has to be qualified almost at once: "Nevertheless, the tank losses in the nineteen days of the Yom Kippur War were about twice those of the World War II battle of El Alamein."[6]

It should be noted that some disparity in the figures on losses on both sides has appeared in written accounts of the war. Sherman, for example, has noted Israeli losses of 1,854 dead and 1,800 seriously wonded.[7] An estimate of Arab losses—dead only—placed the totals for Egypt and Syria at 8,000 each.[8] But such figures can be largely discounted. In some cases, they had to be estimates: Egypt and Syria have shown continued reluctance to issue realistic, accurate figures on losses. In other cases, accounts were prepared in such haste that no official figures were available, forcing guesswork.

Estimates have been made of the dollar costs of the 1967 and 1973 wars for Israel.

The 1967 war cost Israel an estimated $100 million per

day. The October 1973 war apparently cost Israel about $250 million per day, or a total of approximately $6 billion. Israel's total defense imports in 1973 were 1 billion 800 million dollars, or eleven times more than they were in 1966. These arms imports amounted to one-third of everything Israel imported in 1973. Last year Israel spent the astonishing total of 40% of its gross national product on defense.[9]

Summarizing with hindsight, the nineteen days of fighting produced totally new equations in the Middle East. Until time produces answers to those equations, until history provides the essential final findings, it will remain difficult to say with certainty who really emerged the victor. Several factors must be considered.

The Egyptian Army redeemed itself on the field of battle to a degree no one could have predicted; to a somewhat lesser extent, Syria's troops also helped restore Arab pride in the fighting qualities of Arab soldiers. One exception to the latter generalization was Syrian tankers.

> . . . The standard of the tank crews was very low. Like all Arab armies, they never departed from the doctrine implanted in them, and when the situations for which they were not prepared arose, they proved in general to be at a loss.[10]

In the process of proving their valor, the Arab soldiery accomplished two other things. First, this soldiery "shattered the myth of Israeli invincibility."[11] Second, the Egyptian and Syrian troops in particular showed a "grasp of military technology" that induced in Israel "a shock akin to the post-Sputnik trauma in the United States."[12]

In emerging a survivor, the young Israeli state—it marked its twenty-fifth birthday in 1973—assured its continued viability. But Arab, and especially Egyptian, arms not only survived without experiencing a major disaster; they also came, after the war, to believe they had won. Government propaganda helped to produce that euphoric effect, in the process raising the specter of a future revanchist movement that would make the Israelis a target yet again at some point in the future. The Israel Defense Forces had not "broken the bones" of the enemies' military machine so effectively as to discourage a renewal of Arab belligerence.[13]

Internationally, Israel was left more isolated than ever. France, Great Britain, and some other European countries roundly criticized Israel for the intransigence that had rendered impossible any meaningful concessions. Other fallout was reported:

> By the year's end, some 25 [actually twenty-eight] African states had broken diplomatic relations with Israel. They included long-standing allies as Ethiopia, Gambia, and Togo, recipients of substantial Israeli technical and financial aid.[14]

Israel came out of the war with its economy badly out of joint. "[T]he Israeli economy seemed to have little chance of a rapid recovery,"[15] and the war had so dislocated the wheels of industry that factories producing consumer goods closed down and nearly all construction stopped. There occurred many other peripheral results:

> Factories designated as essential, such as those turning out military supplies, or food, were kept going and given preferential treatment. . . . Israeli industry was handicapped by an acute shortage of road transport because so many vehicles had been commandeered by the Army. Potash exports, which depended on huge lorries moving from the Dead Sea to the Port of Ashdod, had to be discontinued, and the transport of citrus fruits was seriously hampered. Many factory managers could not get materials tied up in stores almost round the corner from their plants, or could not shift the products piling up in the warehouses. Imports and raw materials arriving at Israel's ports during the War were discharged in substantial quantities, but the process slowed as the fighting dragged on. Port warehouses were clogged and ships waited in the harbors because the flow of goods was held up for lack of transport.[16]

Many other effects could be noted. But the point is clear. In some ways, because Israel could ill afford heavy losses and manpower, the relative cost to the Israelis was greater than to the Arabs.

The Arabs, as noted, have put the best possible interpretation on the war. Whether realistically or not, they have maintained that they gained their political objectives and kept their armies from disintegrating. In making such claims, they posit the assumption that their military *and* their political aims were limited in nature. Some debate has taken place on that score, as already noted. There has been little or no debate on the reality of the new image of the Arab fighting man. Even Sharon acknowledged that a change had taken place. "I have been fighting for 25 years," Sharon is quoted as saying, "and all the rest were just battles. This was a real war."[17]

The Arab claims may conveniently overlook one entire set of "what if" tactical and purely military possibilities.

> If Sharon had managed to get the Israeli bridge across the Canal on schedule, Egypt would have had difficulty in "maintaining the largest bulk of its forces. . . ." Given another 36 hours, Bren Adan's tanks would have consummated the destruction of the Third Army. Had the Israelis been willing to take more casualties, they could possibly have cut off the Second Army to the north as well.[18]

Then again, the Egyptian First Army could have resealed the canal and assured the destruction of the bulk of Israeli armor by denying its appetite for fuel.

That Egypt and Israel could negotiate with one another after the war may, however, emerge as the most historically significant aspect of the entire war and postwar scenes. Negotiation implies at least de facto recognition. Negotiation also, in the normal case, suggests the possibility of detente, of reconciliation.

President Sadat had this in mind when he made his historic trip to Israel to address the Knesset in November 1977. A year later, agreements for an Israeli-Egyptian peace treaty and Israeli withdrawal from the Sinai were negotiated. Egyptian diplomacy had, by May 1982, recovered the Sinai, opened the Israeli-Egyptian border, and courted U.S. friendship through a series of joint military exercises.

THE REFUGEES

The United Nations Security Council adopted Resolution 242 on 22 November 1967. In it, the Security Council reaffirmed its "concern with the grave situation in the Middle East" and emphasized the "inadmissibility of the acquisition territory by war. . . ."[19] Paragraph 2b of the resolution stated the need to achieve a "just settlement of the refugee problem."[20]

The Security Council resolution that followed the Six-Day War of 1967 proved again that expressions of intent do not necessarily bear results. The refugee problems that had existed in 1967 still existed in 1973, and in a form so virulent that genuine solutions seemed beyond rational expectation. The refugees were the 2.5 million Palestinian Arabs who had fled their homes with the establishment of the state of Israel and who still lived outside or inside Israel's boundaries. Some 400,000 lived in Syria and Lebanon, and about 600,000 in Jordan. Most of the refugees had fled during the 1948–1949 war; the remainder left in 1967. Many have become adjusted to life as citizens of Israel.

These were the refugees who felt with some justification that the Yom Kippur War was theirs, that the Arab states had banded together to win back their homes. Such a natural feeling hardly comported with realities. The Arab states had far more proximate concerns when they launched their coordinated attack on the Day of Atonement. They were extending to the battlefield the policies aimed in the overall weakening or destruction of Israel: so much is true. But they were also trying to redeem their honor, improve their military and political postures, and recapture their own lost territory.

All this implies that the Arab states, in particular Egypt and Syria, felt themselves to be under pressure from Israel. Since Israel's declaration of independence in 1948, that new factor on the Mideast scene had moved steadily out from its originally tiny base until it virtually threatened rival capitals. Especially after the 1967 war, Israel had taken control of territories that gave it little added material wealth but vastly added to its prestige and its defense capabilities. If that process were allowed to continue, some Arab states would soon be Israeli satellites.

Such thinking on the part of the Arab participants in the war excludes the Palestinian Arabs as a major, immediate factor. But it accurately describes Arab thinking. On the latter point, one can quote Azzan Pasha, who said in 1960 while serving as secretary-general of the Arab League:

We have a secret weapon which we can use better than

guns and machine guns, and this is time. As long as we do not make peace with the Zionists, the War is not over; and as long as the War is not over, there is neither victor or vanquished. As soon as we recognize the State of Israel, we admit by this act that we are vanquished.[21]

The war, in other words, could not end. It still had not ended in 1973 when Arab rage, tempered by another bitterly unsuccessful clash (in 1967) with Israel, erupted again into full-scale war.

The small-scale war, it should be stressed, had never stopped. President Sadat has been quoted as saying, in 1969, "Indeed, there can be no hope of any political solution unless the enemy realizes that we are capable of forcing him to withdraw from the fighting."[22]

In this picture, war and the absolute need to avoid any final admission of defeat drove the Arab states on. The original pawns in the game of power, the Palestinians, had been relegated to secondary positions. Israeli success in war had given the Arabs much more to think of than the restoration of displaced persons to their ancestral territories.

Yet the refugees hungered for restoration of a Palestinian nation that existed until Britain and the UN summarily dismembered it under pressure of the World Zionist Organization. They also could teach their children to hunger:

> Eight-year-old Rashid is typical of the children growing up in the [Palestinian Arab] camp (in Jordan). "I am from Haifa," he said. "My home is in Haifa. I live in a white house by the sea. We have orange groves behind my home." Rashid has never seen Haifa: his family left in 1948.[23]

Thus the torch of irredentism was being passed from generation to generation. That in the years after the Yom Kippur War this torch, fueled by the hatred born of dwindling hopes, could spawn one act of terrorism after another to the point where the world shrank in horror should not be surprising. Palestinian nationalism has always been there and always burned passionately. The flames have only risen in direct proportion to the degree to which the Arab states have seemed to accept the permanent existence of an Israeli nation.

Diplomats and soldiers have recognized that the developments of 1973 contributed substantially to a revived and revised Palestinian effort to make good Arab claims to at least some of the lands embraced by the state of Israel. Where once the Palestinian cry had been for restoration of all the old World War I mandate territory of Palestine, by the end of 1973 a change had taken place. The Palestinian leaders, speaking through the Palestine Liberation Organization, had gone on record as being amenable to any substantial portion of Israeli territory. That meant, of course, the Gaza Strip and the West Bank area north, east, and south of Jerusalem.

What had occasioned the downward revision of Palestinian Arab ambitions? The facts of life: "If Sadat had failed in his last military attempt to force Israel to make concessions, then the last chance to reestablish a coastal Palestinian state in place of Israel had effectively failed with it."[24]

And if the downward-scaled ambitions were also dashed? In the opinion of many, that has occurred, and the world is watching the results: machine-gun raids on kibbutzes, bombs in the luggage compartments of Israeli planes, kidnappings and exploding postcards and subversion. The Palestinian refugee, like the earlier Jewish Irgun and Stern Gang, had become a terrorist:

> Since 1967, the image of the Palestinian has changed from "refugee" to "nationalist" and emphasis has shifted from individual rights to repatriation and compensation to national rights and establishment of a Palestinian state. But the refugee problem remains unsolved.[25]

A real solution to "the Palestinian Arab question" will probably remain forever unattainable, short of abandonment or the collapse of Israel. Even then, disagreements among Arab leaders would no doubt give rise to new and equally permanent and equally bloody differences. A straw in the wind may be the reactions of East- and West-Bank Arabs to a Jordanian-PLO suggestion that the West Bank become an independent Arab entity leagued in some sort of federation with Jordan. Where East-Bank Arabs seemed basically to favor such a proposal, those on the West Bank seemed equally hostile to it: they did not, it appeared, want their capital in Ammon.

The intensity of such feeling cannot be measured because the plan has never even been conceived. It remains one of many broached and forgotten. Under any circumstance, it could not survive without Israeli sanction, and that has never been forthcoming. Thus after 1973, the question continued to thunder across the Mideast: how to pull the poisonous fangs of the Palestinian Arab movement—if, in fact, those fangs can be extracted?

The answer to that question depended largely on Israel, and Israel, expectably, began after the Yom Kippur War to pursue its own security needs first. Security became the prime concern, a concern that drove Israel yet into another war in Lebanon.

In June 1982, Israeli troops attacked Palestinian positions in southern Lebanon in operation "Peace for Galilee." In Lebanon, the Palestinian refugee population had swollen to a half million. The PLO used the refugee camps to recruit and train terrorists for harassment attacks into Israel. In March 1978, Israeli forces attacked and destroyed these PLO bases. In June, the Israelis withdrew with the arrival of a six-thousand-man UN peacekeeping force and the establishment of a Christian militia zone known as Haddad Land.

The arming of PLO forces with long-range artillery, 130mm howitzers, and BM-21 Katyusha rocket launchers that fired over the zones into Galilee provoked Israel into the 1982 operation. The Israeli army not only began with tacit approval from Egypt and Jordan, but for the first time fought alongside Arab allies, the Lebanese Christian Militias. In a three-pronged attack supported by air superiority and amphibious landings, the Israeli Defense Forces quickly established their offensive objective of a twenty-five-mile buffer zone in southern Lebanon.

Military operations continued northward at the urging of Defense Minister Ariel Sharon. The decision to move north ranks as Israel's biggest political mistake. The moderate Arabs moved to distance themselves, convinced other Arabs of Israeli trickery, and demonstrated American loss of leverage over Israeli actions.

Sharon's plan to annihilate the PLO, kick out the Syrians, and establish a non-Moslem, pro-Israel Lebanon crumbled at the gates of Beirut. The Israeli blitzkrieg bogged down into a medieval siege. West Beirut was bombarded for ten weeks.

Israel finally bowed to internal and international pressure for settlement. A peacekeeping force of Americans, French, and Italians oversaw the PLO withdrawal from the city. In the finest British tradition, PLO Leader Yassir Arafat had used the media to turn a military defeat into a political victory.

Israel had gained not only the southern half of Lebanon but a state of destabilization associated with the mosaic of feuding religious and political militias. These militias forced the peacekeepers out, and, in sum, Israel again lost more than it gained. One of the world's most militarily competent nations ironically is proving to be one of the world's most politically incompetent.

LESSONS LEARNED

The lessons of the Yom Kippur War and the new realities it generated lie in the military arena. The war never had the immediate purpose of solving the Palestinian Arab problem, nor, perhaps, could it have done so even if that had been its goal. One can summarize the war in terms of what it taught.

The tank is alive and well and still important in warfare despite reports of its demise. That holds particularly true, of course, where the terrain makes possible rapid movements and maneuver. Notably, in one instance at least, "... in the battle in the Sinai the Israeli Defense Forces fought exclusively with tanks against five infantry divisions and performed at one and the same time the tasks of defense, holding the front line, and of counterattack."[26]

The tank cannot be emphasized to the exclusion of infantry and artillery, and particularly not to the exclusion of missiles and air power. All have to work together in an orchestrated and balanced weapon and manpower system. For the Israeli Defense Forces, the lack of infantry and artillery became especially embarrassing in the Sinai battles, literally forcing local commanders to over-rely on armor with occasional key help from specialized infantry such as paratroops and commandos.

Israel's army has taken the balanced-force lesson to heart more than have the Arab military establishments. The IDF found itself seriously handicapped in some situations because of lack of balance:

> Tremendous investment was made in air and armor, while below in the field there was a lack of fire power, mortars, flame-throwers, night-fighting equipment, and adequate mobility. Israeli ground forces ... were still based on arms of service with their loyalties and their pressure groups and their positions in planning conferences.[27]

In the area of intelligence, the modern army requires the very best that can be provided at every level. "Every level," in this instance, means any point in the hierarchy of sources of information and data from which useful facts may be gleaned, from enemy headquarters to battlefield reconnaissance such as that which alerted the Israeli southern command to the gap between the Egyptian Second and Third armies.

Obtaining intelligence represents only the first step, however. A second requires digestion and interpretation, and a third involves application. Decisions are essential if intelligence is to be of value. Taking a realistic look at its conduct of the war, the Egyptian high command may focus on this aspect of its operations. The decision to play down the Israeli crossing of the canal, whether or not based on faulty intelligence, opened the door to disaster.

The enemy should never be underestimated. Both the Arabs and the Israelis made the mistake at different times of incorrectly measuring their opponents. In both cases, the erroneous assessments were carried out in terms of false assumptions or preconceptions, and each time the error brought grave consequences. At the beginning of the war, the Israelis misread the Arab armies' capability for attack. Near the war's end, the Egyptians, basking in their early successes and anesthetized by them, allowed the canal bridgehead to become a virtually full-scale invasion of Egyptian soil.

Such are the lessons of the war, a struggle fought almost under laboratory conditions for extremely high stakes. It may be noted that most of the battles took place in desert or lightly populated terrain. That factor alone enabled the commands and front-line officers to concentrate almost totally on the combat problems facing them.

The Yom Kippur War provided examples of almost unparalleled heroism. It is to be hoped that the war also contributed its very valuable need to what may be long-term stabilization of the political and ideological cauldron that is the Middle East. But even if that had not been so, the war would still be worth studying because of its tactical aspects. Life and death hung in the balance as the armies maneuvered and the tanks rolled, as in all wars. In this one, however, all the factors essential to the creation of a test-tube situation seemed to combine.

Some of the factors have been noted. The war opened with shock and retreat on the Israeli side. A very brief period of recovery and mobilization preceded the counterattack in the north. Once that front had been stabilized, the southern front became the main theater of action. There again the armies stood at bay briefly before the lightning moves began that led to superpower and UN Security Council decisions and, finally, to a truce.

One can note that none of the major participants in the war was overmatched to any great degree, at least until the final hours. None struck and won without cost, thought, or effort. Thus the war becomes all the more a paradigm for study.

On the Egyptian side, as noted earlier, the officer corps had once been elitist to the bone. Changes were being made at the time of the Yom Kippur War, but they had not yet become a way of life, and might not for a long time. The chain-of-command structure basically reflected social realities in Egyptian life.

The consequences of defeat, in part from a lack of strategic time and space, has by necessity molded a breed of soldier in Israel with a common resolve to survive. The Israeli soldier again proved that he could function effectively on attack. In that type of situation, the soldier, and his lower- and middle-echelon superiors, must employ wit and intelligence, and utilize flexibility if he is to carry it off at all. Those characteristics grow naturally in a society that teaches its young, "Don't just stand there, do something!"

None of this was peripheral to the war itself. All of it was focal.

The tactical facts of the war are on the records. The political hope of the postwar future is still to be fulfilled. The outlook, however, does not hold promise for future Arab-Israeli cooperation.

The Israeli 1982 operation, with Tolstoyan form, evolved out of control into an overt invasion of Lebanon. Israel suffered a credibility loss with the moderate Arab states and tensions with Syria reached war footing. Another Mideast conflict would have certainly been provoked had Iraq and Iran not already been at war and the multinational peacekeeping force not intervened. Presently the peacekeeping force has been withdrawn and the dispersed Palestinians are returning and regrouping in Syria and Lebanon. The elements of confrontation are present and inevitable, awaiting a spark to set it off.

APPENDIX A
MAPS

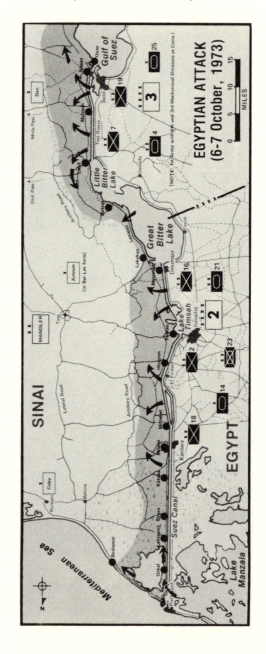

ISRAELI COUNTERATTACK
(8 OCTOBER 1973)

ISRAELI COUNTERATTACK
(15 OCTOBER 1973)

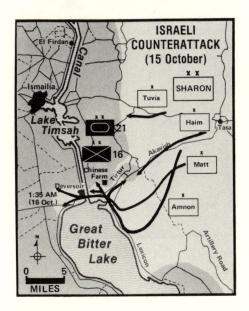

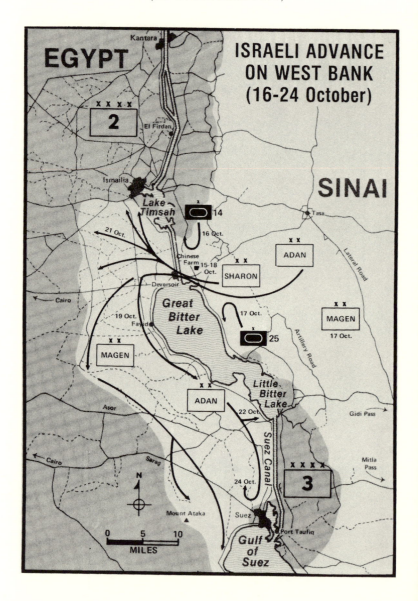

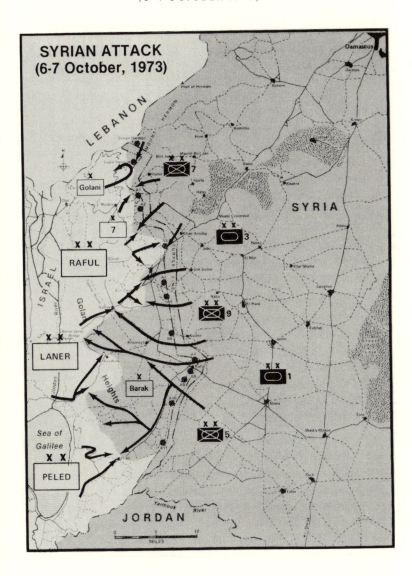

SYRIAN ATTACK
(6-7 October, 1973)

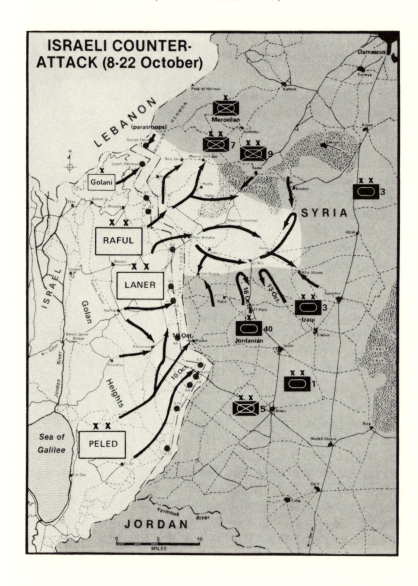

APPENDIX B
ILLUSTRATIONS

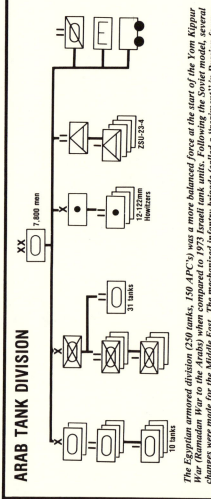

ARAB TANK DIVISION

xx
7,800 men

10 tanks

31 tanks

12-122mm Howitzers

ZSU-23-4

The Egyptian armored division (250 tanks, 150 APC's) was a more balanced force at the start of the Yom Kippur War (Ramadan War to the Arabs) when compared to 1973 Israeli tank units. Following the Soviet model, several changes were made for the Middle East. The mechanized infantry brigade (called a "regiment" in Russian formations) included a battalion of tanks, while anti-tank (AT) weapons were liberally distributed among the infantry: Sagger AT missiles at brigade-level; recoilless rifles at battalion-level; and RPG-7 (rocket propelled grenade) at platoon-level. Whereas the Israeli tank units were to be committed immediately at the start of hostilities, the Egyptian armored divisions (two had been organized for the War) true to Soviet doctrine were not to become engaged until several days after the bridgeheads on the east bank were established.

ISRAELI TANK BRIGADE

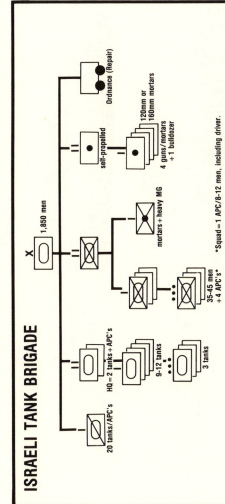

1,850 men

20 tanks/APC's

HQ = 2 tanks + APC's

9-12 tanks

3 tanks

35-45 men
+ 4 APC's*

mortars + heavy MG

self-propelled

120mm or
160mm mortars

4 guns/mortars
+1 bulldozer

Ordnance (Repair)

*Squad = 1 APC/8-12 men, including driver.

In both the Six-Day and Yom Kippur Wars the basic unit of the I.D.F. was the brigade (CHATIVAH). In the 1967 War the I.D.F. had time to organize and deploy their forces according to a set plan. Most tank brigades therefore appeared as shown above. 2-3 brigades were grouped together under an UGDAH (literally "task force") and this divisional structure had become standardized by the 1973 War. Each of these UGDAHS or Tank Divisions had its own reconnaissance unit, nine self-propelled artillery batteries (155mm guns or 160mm mortars), as well as engineer, ordnance (repair), and anti-aircraft units. The I.D.F. did not have time to bring all of their formations to battle in 1973 as complete units. Platoons (MACHLAKAH), companies (PLUGAH), and battalions (GDUD) were fed piecemeal to the fronts, formed into ad hoc units or distributed among the brigades already there. Adding to this general disorganization was the neglect of the armored infantry between the wars. While most mechanized in-fantry units' M.3 halftracks had been replaced with newer U.S. M.113 APC's, in 1973 many tank brigades had 2-3 tank battalions only and no infantry component. (Sometimes even the brigade artillery was missing.) To rectify this, by the second week of the Yom Kippur War a mechanized infantry company was assigned to each tank battalion (replacing the 4th tank company). Even this proved insufficient and more infantry (including paratroops) were attached to the brigades.

MAIN BATTLE TANKS, 1973

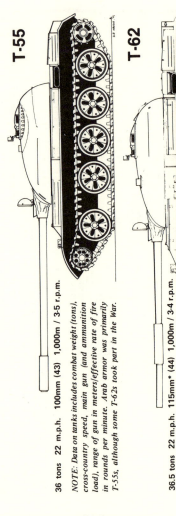

T-55

36 tons   22 m.p.h.   100mm (43)   1,000m / 3-5 r.p.m.

NOTE: Data on tanks includes combat weight (tons), cross-country speed, main gun (and ammunition load), range of gun in meters/effective rate of fire in rounds per minute. Arab armor was primarily T-55s, although some T-62s took part in the War.

T-62

36.5 tons   22 m.p.h.   115mm* (44)   1,000m / 3-4 r.p.m.

*The 115mm gun is smoothbore, with a sophisticated fin-stabilized armor piercing round. But lack of good range-finding optics eliminated any theoretical advantage Soviet tanks had over their Western counterparts.

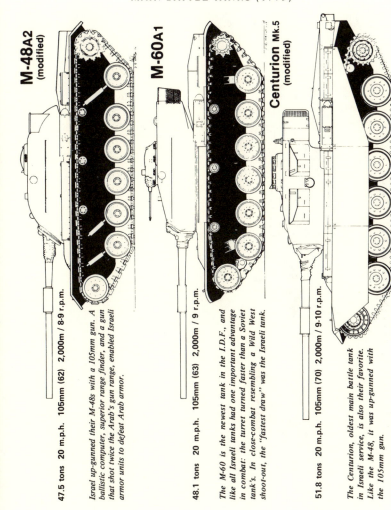

M-48A2 (modified)

47.5 tons   20 m.p.h.   105mm (62)   2,000m / 8-9 r.p.m.

Israel up-gunned their M-48s with a 105mm gun. A ballistic computer, superior range finder, and a gun that shot twice the Arab's gun range, enabled Israeli armor units to defeat Arab armor.

M-60A1

48.1 tons   20 m.p.h.   105mm (63)   2,000m / 9 r.p.m.

The M-60 is the newest tank in the I.D.F., and like all Israeli tanks had one important advantage in combat: the turret turned faster than a Soviet tank's. In close-combat resembling a Wild West shoot-out, the "fastest draw" was the Israeli tank.

Centurion Mk.5 (modified)

51.8 tons   20 m.p.h.   105mm (70)   2,000m / 9-10 r.p.m.

The Centurion, oldest main battle tank in Israeli service, is also their favorite. Like the M-48, it was up-gunned with the 105mm gun.

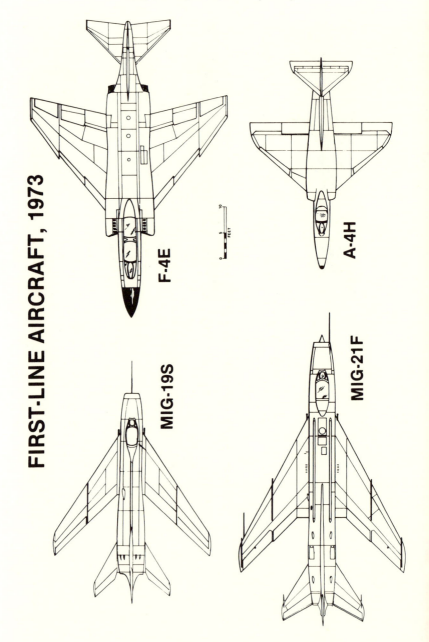

FIRST-LINE AIRCRAFT, 1973

F-4E

A-4H

MIG-19S

MIG-21F

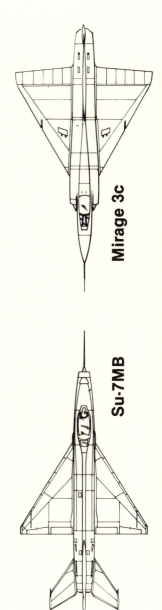

Mirage 3c

Su-7MB

	MIG-19S	MIG-21F	Su-7MB	F-4E	A-4H	Mirage 3c
Maximum Speed	846 m.p.h.	1,386 m.p.h.	1,056 m.p.h.	1,386 m.p.h.	675 m.p.h.	1,386 m.p.h.
Service Ceiling	55,000 ft.	59,055 ft.	42,000 ft.	62,000 ft.	47,900 ft.	59,000 ft.
Combat Radius	280 miles	340 miles	180 miles	550 miles	290 miles	180 miles
Armament	3—30mm cannon	1—30mm cannon	2—30mm cannon	1—20mm cannon	2—20mm cannon	2—30mm cannon
Payload (bombs, rockets, etc.)	and up to 1,100 lbs.	and up to 2,200 lbs.	and up to 5,000 lbs.	and up to 16,000 lbs.	and up to 8,200 lbs.	and up to 2,000 lbs.

Note: Only the most numerous types of aircraft employed during the War are listed above. Many planes in both sides' inventory never engaged in combat (such as the MIG-23 and MIG-25). The Israeli-built Barak fighter is comparable to the Mirage 3c. The maximum speeds listed are for "clean" aircraft—without their load of missiles or bombs.

ARAB MISSILE BOATS, 1973

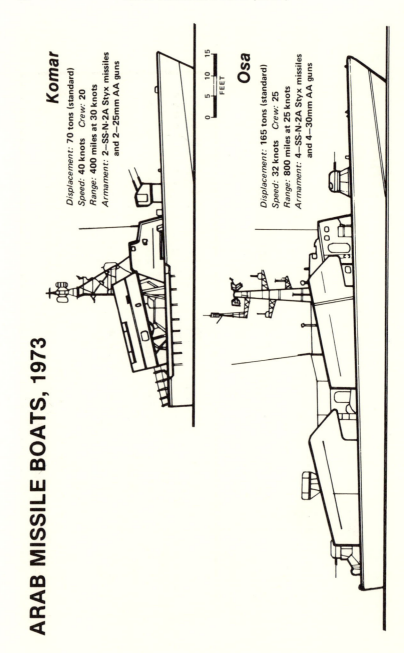

Komar

Displacement: **70 tons (standard)**
Speed: **40 knots**   *Crew:* **20**
Range: **400 miles at 30 knots**
Armament: **2–SS-N-2A Styx missiles
and 2–25mm AA guns**

Osa

Displacement: **165 tons (standard)**
Speed: **32 knots**   *Crew:* **25**
Range: **800 miles at 25 knots**
Armament: **4–SS-N-2A Styx missiles
and 4–30mm AA guns**

0   5   10   15
FEET

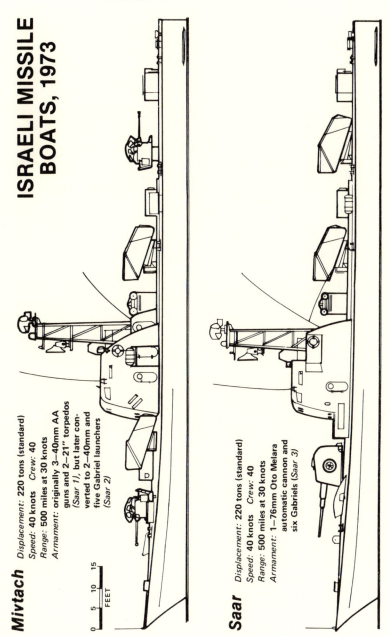

ISRAELI MISSILE BOATS, 1973

Mivtach *Displacement:* **220 tons (standard)**
Speed: **40 knots**   *Crew:* **40**
Range: **500 miles at 30 knots**
Armament: **originally 3—40mm AA
guns and 2—21" torpedoes
(*Saar 1*), but later con-
verted to 2—40mm and
five Gabriel launchers
(*Saar 2*)**

Saar *Displacement:* **220 tons (standard)**
Speed: **40 knots**   *Crew:* **40**
Range: **500 miles at 30 knots**
Armament: **1—76mm Oto Melara
automatic cannon and
six Gabriels (*Saar 3*)**

0 5 10 15
FEET

APPENDIX C
ORDERS OF BATTLE

ISRAELI ORDER OF BATTLE
OCTOBER 1973

Israel fought the Yom Kippur War with 37 brigades: 10 armored, 9 mechanized, 9 infantry, 5 parachute, and 3 artillery. Brigades were assigned to divisions based upon their combat tasks. Names in parentheses are nicknames acquired as young officers in keeping with the Israeli practice of limiting identification below the staff command level.

Northern Command	Major General Hoffi
Mechanized Division	Brigadier General (Raful) Eytan
Armored Division	Major General Laner
Armored Division	Major General (Mussa) Peled
Central Command	Major General Ephrant
Composite Division	
Southern Command	Major General (Gorodish) Gonen (replaced 10 October by Lieutenant General Bar-Lev)
Armored Division	Major General (Albert) Mandler (killed in action 13 October; replaced by Brigadier General Magen)
Armored Division	Major General (Bren) Adan
Armored Division	Major General (Arik) Sharon
Composite Division	Brigadier General Magen (replaced 13 October by Brigadier General Yzhaki)
Composite Division	Colonel Granit (replaced 15 October by Brigadier General Meron)

Shlomo Command		Major General (Shaike) Gavish
Composite Division		
Air Force		Major General Peled
Fighters	352	
Bombers	8	
Transports	66	
Helicopters	50	
Navy		Rear Admiral Telem
Fast Attack Boats	51	
Submarines	2	

(Rein) units have an armored brigade attached; (Minus) units have an armored brigade detached.

First Army (Reserve)	Lieutenant General Shazli (replaced 20 October by Major General Gamasy)
Third Mechanized Division (Minus)	Brigadier Nelgati
Sixth Mechanized Division	Brigadier Moharram
14 brigades:	
6 commando	
2 air mobile	
1 parachute	
3 armored	
2 artillery	
Second Army	Major General Mamoun (replaced 14 October by Major General Khalil)
Second Infantry Division (Rein)	Brigadier Saada
Sixteenth Infantry Division (Rein)	Brigadier Hafiz
Eighteenth Infantry Division (Rein)	Brigadier Ghaly
Twenty-third Mechanized Infantry Division (Minus)	Brigadier Latif
Twenty-first Armored Division (Minus)	Brigadier Orabi
Second Army Artillery Division	Brigadier Ghazala
5 brigades:	
1 mechanized infantry	
1 infantry	
1 parachute	
1 commando	
1 engineer	
Third Army	Major General Wassel
Seventh Infantry Division (Rein)	Brigadier Zumur
Nineteenth Infantry Division (Rein)	Brigadier Afifi
Fourth Armored Division (Minus)	Brigadier Kabil

Third Army Artillery Division		Brigadier Shasli
4 brigades:		
1 mechanized		
infantry		
1 amphibious		
1 commando		
1 engineer		

Red Sea Command
  3 brigades:
    2 infantry
    1 commando

Air Force		Major General Mubarak
Fighters	550	
Bombers	48	
Transports	70	
Helicopters	82	

Navy		Vice Admiral Zekry
Fast Attack Boats	60	
Submarines	12	
Destroyers	8	
Amphibious Craft	14	

Air Defense Force		Major General Fahmy
SA-2 (Guideline)	90 batteries	
SA-3 (Goa)	78 batteries	
SA-6 (Gainful)	40 batteries	

		Arrival Date
Algeria	Armored Brigade	24 October
	3 Aircraft Squadrons	9–11 October
Iraq	1 Aircraft Squadron	11 October
Kuwait	Yarmuk Infantry Brigade	In Egypt
Libya	Armored Brigade	In Egypt
	2 Aircraft Squadrons	In Egypt
Morocco	Infantry Brigade	8 October
North Yemen	Island Garrisons	14 October
Palestine Liberation	Ain Jalloud Brigade	In Egypt
Army	Commando Brigade	In Egypt
Pakistan	Field Ambulance Unit	10 October
South Yemen	3 Landing Craft	6 October
The Sudan	Infantry Battalion	28 October
Tunisia	Infantry Battalion	18 October

(Rein) units have an armored brigade attached; (Mechanized) units are not completely converted to mechanized.

Syrian Army	Major General Chakour
First Armored Division	Colonel Jehne
Third Armored Division	Brigadier Sharba
Fifth (Mechanized) Infantry Division (Rein)	Brigadier Aslan
Seventh (Mechanized) Infantry Division (Rein)	Brigadier Abrash (killed in action 8 October; replaced 9 October by Brigadier Berakdar)
Ninth (Mechanized) Infantry Division (Rein)	Colonel Tourkmani

Reserves

12 brigades:
3 armored
1 mechanized infantry
6 infantry
1 commando
1 parachute

Navy		Rear Admiral Hussein
Fast Attack Boats	25	

Air Force		Major General Jamil
Fighters	275	
Transports	16	
Helicopters	36	
SA-2 (Guideline)	8 batteries	
SA-3 (Goa)	17 batteries	
SA-6 (Gainful)	10 batteries	

ARAB ALLIES WITH SYRIA

		Arrival Date
Iraq	Third Armored Division	11 October
	Sixth Armored Division (Minus)	11 October
	Special Forces Brigade	11 October
	3 Aircraft Squadrons	8–11 October
Jordan	Third Armored Division (Minus)	13–23 October
Kuwait	Artillery Battery	14 October
Morocco	Mechanized Brigade	In Syria
Pakistan	Field Ambulance Unit	10 October
Saudi Arabia	Twentieth Infantry Brigade	14 October

NOTES

CHAPTER 1: BACKGROUND TO WAR

1. American Friends Service Committee, *After the October War* (Philadelphia: American Friends Service Committee, 1974), p. 1.
2. American Friends Service Committee, *Major Powers in the Middle East* (Philadelphia: American Friends Service Committee, 1974), p. 1.
3. American Friends Service Committee, *Search for Peace in the Middle East* (Philadelphia: American Friends Service Committee, 1970), p. 2.
4. *Encyclopaedia Britannica*, Book of the Year 1968, "The 1967 Arab-Israeli War," by R. E. Hue, p. 276.
5. *After the October War*, p. 3.
6. Ibid., p. 2.
7. Insight Team (the *London Sunday Times*), *The Yom Kippur War* (New York: Doubleday, 1974), p. 312.
8. Walter Laqueur, *Confrontation: The Middle East and World Politics* (New York: Quadrangle Books, 1974), pp. 3, 98.
9. Insight Team, p. 169.
10. Merrill Sheila with Lloyd H. Norman, "Israel's DEW Line in the Sinai," *Newsweek*, 28 July, 1975, p. 26.
11. *Aviation Week & Space Technology*, 3 December 1973, p. 19.
12. Samuel Katz, *Battleground Fact and Fantasy in Palestine* (New York: Bantam Books, 1973), pp. 164, 165.
13. Arnold Sherman, *When God Judged and Men Died* (New York: Bantam Books, 1973), p. 11.
14. Insight Team, p. 307.
15. Ibid., p. 306.
16. Ibid., p. 28.
17. Peter Allen, *The Yom Kippur War* (New York: Charles Scribner's Sons, 1982), p. 21.
18. Insight Team, p. 66.
19. Katz, p. 131.

20. Laqueur, p. 82.
21. Ibid., p. 46.
22. The *Koran*, 2:190.

CHAPTER 2: OPENING MOVES

1. Sherman, p. 27.
2. Laqueur, p. 85.
3. Insight Team, p. 134.
4. Laqueur, p. 102.
5. Insight Team, pp. 134, 157.
6. Ibid., p. 159.
7. Saad el Shazly, *The Crossing of the Suez* (San Francisco: American Mideast Research, 1980), p. 222.
8. Insight Team, p. 139.
9. Ibid.
10. Desmond Young, *Rommel: The Desert Fox* (New York: Berkley Publishing Corp., 1952), p. 225.
11. *Aviation Week & Space Technology*, 3 December 1973, p. 18.
12. Ibid., p. 22.
13. Insight Team, p. 161.
14. *Aviation Week & Space Technology*, 3 December 1973, p. 15.
15. Sherman, pp. 47–50.
16. Insight Team, p. 141.
17. Ibid.
18. *Aviation Week & Space Technology*, 3 December 1973, p. 21.
19. Sherman, p. 30.
20. Ibid., p. 27.
21. Hassel el Badri, et al., *The Ramadan War, 1973* (Dunn Loring, Virginia: T. N. Dupuy Associates, 1978), pp. 64–65.
22. Ibid., pp. 161–62.
23. Insight Team, p. 72.
24. Charles J. V. Murphy, "The Airlift that Saved Israel," *Reader's Digest*, July 1974, pp. 86–90.
25. Ibid.

CHAPTER 3: MISSILES GO TO WAR

1. Insight Team, p. 154.
2. A. J. Barker, *The Yom Kippur War* (New York: Ballantine Books, 1974), p. 69.
3. Ibid., pp. 75–78.
4. Insight Team, p. 184.
5. Ibid., p. 167.
6. Chaim Herzog, *The War of Atonement: October 1973* (Boston: Little, Brown, 1975), p. 258.

7. Ibid., p. 259.
8. Sherman, p. 30.
9. Laqueur, pp. 105–8.
10. Insight Team, p. 194.
11. Ibid., p. 195.
12. Barker, *The Yom Kippur War*, pp. 96–97.
13. Insight Team, p. 198.
14. *Aviation Week & Space Technology*, 17 December 1973, pp. 15–16.
15. Sherman, pp. 46–47.
16. Trevor N. Dupuy, *Elusive Victory: The Arab-Israeli Wars, 1947–1974* (New York: Harper & Row, 1978), p. 595.
17. *Aviation Week & Space Technology*, 17 December 1973, p. 17.
18. *Aviation Week & Space Technology*, 5 November 1973, p. 17, and 22 October 1973, p. 21.
19. Insight Team (Missile Pictorial Section), n.p.
20. U.S. *News and World Report*, 17 March 1975, p. 16.
21. Insight Team, pp. 213–14.
22. Ibid., pp. 411–12.

CHAPTER 4: WAR IN THE AIR

1. Insight Team, p. 42.
2. Ibid., pp. 110, 111.
3. Ibid., p. 119.
4. Ibid., p. 120.
5. *Aviation Week & Space Technology*, 3 December 1973, p. 18.
6. Herzog, *The War of Atonement*, p. 57.
7. Ibid., p. 254.
8. Ibid., p. 260.
9. Sherman, pp. 22, 23.
10. Ibid., pp. 25, 26.
11. Ibid., p. 27.
12. Ibid., p. 37.
13. *Aviation Week & Space Technology*, 17 December 1973, pp. 15, 16.
14. Ibid., p. 16.
15. Insight Team, p. 311.
16. Sherman, pp. 33, 34.
17. Kent Clotfelter, "The Yom Kippur War, October 6–24, 1973," *Wargamer's Digest*, May 1974, p. 11.
18. Laqueur, pp. 132, 133.
19. Insight Team, p. 437.
20. *Aviation Week & Space Technology*, 3 December 1973, p. 18.

CHAPTER 5: DESERT WARRIORS AT SEA

1. Martin J. Miller, Jr., "The Israeli Navy: 26 Years of Non-Peace," U.S. *Naval Institute Proceedings* 101, No. 2/864 (February 1975): 48–54.

2. Laqueur, p. 2.

3. David C. Isby and James F. Dunnigan, "Sixth Fleeet US/Soviet Naval Operations in the Mediterranean in the 1970s," *Strategy & Tactics* (January/February 1975), p. 8.

4. Shazli, pp. 23–24.

5. Sherman, p. 41.

6. M. J. Miller, "The Israeli Navy," p. 53.

7. Sherman, pp. 62–63.

8. Dupuy, p. 561.

9. M. J. Miller, "The Israeli Navy," p. 54.

10. Ibid.

11. Isby and Dunnigan, p. 9.

12. Shlomo Slonim, "Suez and the Soviets," U.S. *Naval Institute Proceedings* 101, No. 4/866 (April 1975): 36–41.

13. Ibid., p. 37.

14. Ibid., p. 38.

15. Ibid., p. 39.

16. Alfred T. Mahan, *The Influence of Seapower upon History* 1660–1783 (New York: Hill & Wang, 1957), pp. 20–21.

17. Lt. (j.g.) F. C. Miller, "Those Storm-beaten Ships, Upon Which the Arab Armies Never Looked," U.S. *Naval Institute Proceedings* 101, No. 3/865 (March 1975): 18–25.

18. Ibid., p. 21.

19. Sherman, p. 83.

20. M. J. Miller, "The Israeli Navy," p. 54.

21. Dupuy, p. 563.

CHAPTER 6: THE HOLDING ACTIONS

1. Sherman, p. 48.

2. Ibid., p. 49.

3. Ibid., pp. 49–50.

4. Insight Team, p. 178.

5. Laqueur, p. 133.

6. Insight Team, p. 178.

7. Ibid., p. 294.

8. Ibid.

9. *Time*, 22 October 1973, p. 38.

10. Ibid.

11. Ibid.

12. Ibid.

13. Sherman, p. 52.

14. *Newsweek*, 22 October 1973, p. 79.

15. Ibid., p. 60.

CHAPTER 7: COUNTERATTACK

1. Dupuy, p. 465.
2. Herzog, *The War of Atonement*, p. 116.
3. Ibid., p. 118.
4. Ibid., p. 120.
5. *Newsweek*, 22 October 1973, p. 79.
6. Herzog, *The War of Atonement*, p. 124.
7. Insight Team, pp. 240, 241.
8. Laqueur, p. 105.
9. Col. Robert J. Hicks (ret.), "The Arab-Israeli War of 1973," *Armor*, December 1973, p. 8.
10. *Newsweek*, 22 October 1973, p. 82.
11. Dupuy, p. 468.
12. Ibid., pp. 535–36.
13. Herzog, *The War of Atonement*, p. 192.
14. Insight Team, p. 192.
15. Ibid., p. 191.
16. Ibid., p. 189.
17. Ibid., p. 207.
18. Ibid.
19. *Newsweek*, 22 October 1973, p. 63.
20. Herzog, *The War of Atonement*, p. 197.
21. Insight Team, p. 243.

CHAPTER 8: FLANKING ATTACK

1. Barker, *The Yom Kippur War*, p. 120.
2. Henry Tanner, "Cairo Says Aim is Retaking Land," *The New York Times*, 16 October 1973, p. 18.
3. J. F. C. Fuller, *The Conduct of War* (Rutgers, N.J.: Rutgers University Press, 1968), p. 44.
4. Laqueur, p. 134.
5. Herzog, *The War of Atonement*, p. 210.
6. Barker, *The Yom Kippur War*, p. 120.
7. Insight Team, p. 327.
8. Ibid., p. 329.
9. Ibid., p. 330.
10. Herzog, *The War of Atonement*, p. 231.
11. Ibid., p. 212.
12. Barker, *The Yom Kippur War*, p. 123.
13. Terence Smith, "Israelis West of Canal Find Burned-Out Zone," *The New York Times*, 22 October 1973, p. 19.
14. Ibid.
15. Herzog, *The War of Atonement*, p. 223.
16. Barker, *The Yom Kippur War*, p. 125.

17. Herzog, *The War of Atonement*, p. 226.
18. Ibid.
19. Insight Team, p. 341.

CHAPTER 9: BREAKTHROUGH AND ENVELOPMENT

1. Herzog, *The War of Atonement*, p. 195.
2. Barker, *The Yom Kippur War*, p. 120.
3. Herzog, *The War of Atonement*, p. 229.
4. Ibid.
5. Ibid., p. 230.
6. Ibid.
7. Ibid., p. 343.
8. Insight Team, p. 342.
9. Ibid., p. 345.
10. Ibid.
11. Simulations Publications, Inc., *Sinai* (New York: S.P.I., 1973), p. 1.
12. Richard Eder, "Arabs Cut Oil Exports 5% a Month," *The New York Times*, 18 October 1973, p. 1.
13. Herzog, *The War of Atonement*, p. 245.
14. Ibid., p. 246.
15. Insight Team, p. 395.
16. Ibid., p. 247.
17. Ibid., p. 249.
18. Ibid., p. 250.
19. Jean Larteguy, *The Walls of Israel* (New York: M. Evans & Co., 1968), p. 208.
20. Peter Allen, *The Yom Kippur War* (New York: Charles Scribner's Sons, 1982), p. 230.
21. Edgar O'Ballance, *No Victor, No Vanquished: The Yom Kippur War* (London, Presidio Press, 1978), p. 259.
22. Ibid., p. 260.

CHAPTER 10: FINAL POSITIONS AND THE FUTURE

1. Barker, *The Yom Kippur War*, p. 137.
2. Sherman, p. 147.
3. Barker, *The Yom Kippur War*, p. 149.
4. Ibid., p. 157.
5. Ibid., p. 155.
6. Ibid.
7. Sherman, p. 147.
8. Insight Team, p. 450.
9. American Friends Service Committee, "Middle East Aspects of the World Arms Race," *Bulletin* (June 1974), pp. 3–4.

10. Herzog, *The War of Atonement*, p. 275.

11. Barker, *The Yom Kippur War*, p. 143.

12. Ibid., pp. 145–46.

13. Ibid., p. 146.

14. Field Enterprises Educational Corporation, *The 1974 World Book Yearbook* (Chicago: Field Enterprises Educational Corp., 1974), p. 404.

15. Insight Team, p. 451.

16. Barker, *The Yom Kippur War*, p. 147.

17. Insight Team, p. 489.

18. Ibid.

19. Majdia D. Khadduri, *The Arab-Israel Impasse* (Washington, D.C.: Robert B. Luce, 1968), p. 223.

20. Ibid.

21. Nadav Safran, *From War to War: The Arab-Israeli Confrontation, 1948–1967* (New York: Pegasus, 1969), p. 39.

22. Herzog, *The War of Atonement*, p. 15.

23. Insight Team, p. 456.

24. Ibid., p. 459.

25. American Friends Service Committee, "A State for the Palestinians?" *Bulletin* (June 1974), p. 3.

26. Herzog, *The War of Atonement*, p. 273.

27. Ibid., p. 272.

LIST OF WORKS
CONSULTED

BOOKS AND ARTICLES

Adan, Avraham. *On the Banks of the Suez*. San Rafael: Presidio Press, 1980.

Allen, Peter. *The Yom Kippur War*. New York: Charles Scribner's Sons, 1982.

American Friends Service Committee. *After the War*. Philadelphia: American Friends Service Committee, 1974.

————. *Major Powers in the Middle East*. Philadelphia: American Friends Service Committee, 1974.

————. "Middle East Aspects of the World Arms Race." *Bulletin* (June 1974).

————. *Search for Peace in the Middle East*. Philadelphia: American Friends Service Committee, 1970.

————. "A State for the Palestinians?" *Bulletin* (June 1974).

Badri, Hassel el, et al. *The Ramadan War, 1973*. Dunn Loring, Virginia: T. N. Dupuy Associates, 1978.

Barker, A. J. *Arab-Israeli Wars*. New York: Hippocrene Books, 1981.

————. *The Yom Kippur War*. New York: Ballantine Books, 1974.

Bradford, George, and Len Morgan. *50 Famous Tanks*. New York: Arco Publishing Co., 1974.

Clotfelter, Kent. "The Yom Kippur War, October 6–24, 1973." *Wargamer's Digest* (May 1974), pp. 9–14.

Davidson, Kerry. *Twentieth-Century Civilization*. New York: Barnes & Noble Books, 1975.

Dupuy, Trevor. *Elusive Victory: The Arab-Israeli Wars, 1947–1974*. New York: Harper & Row, 1978.

Eder, Richard. "Arabs Cut Oil Exports 5% a Month." *The New York Times* (18 October 1973), p. 1.

Field Enterprises Educational Corporation. *The 1974 World Book Yearbook*. Chicago: Field Enterprises Educational Corp., 1974.

Foss, Christopher F. *Jane's Pocket Book of Modern Tanks and Armored Fighting Vehicles*. New York: Collier Books, 1974.

Fuller, J. F. C. *The Conduct of War*. New Brunswick, N.J.: Rutgers University Press, 1968.

Gilbert, Martin. *The Arab-Israeli Conflict: Its History in Maps*. London: Weidenfeld & Nicolson, 1974.

Hart, B. H. Liddell. *Strategy*. New York: Frederick A. Praeger, 1967.

Herzog, Chaim. *The Arab-Israeli Wars: War and Peace in the Middle East*. New York: Random House, 1982.

———. *The War of Atonement: October 1973*. Boston: Little, Brown, 1975.

Hicks, Col. Robert J. (ret.). "The Arab-Israeli War of 1973." *Armor* (December 1973), p. 8.

Insight Team (*The London Sunday Times*). *The Yom Kippur War*. New York: Doubleday, 1974.

International Institute for Strategic Studies. *Strategic Study 1973*. London, 1974.

Isby, David C., and James F. Dunnigan. "Sixth Fleet US/Soviet Naval Operations in the Mediterranean in the 1970s." *Strategy & Tactics* (January/February 1975), p. 8.

Kalb, Marvin. *Kissinger*. Boston: Little, Brown, 1974.

Katz, Samuel. *Battleground: Fact and Fantasy in Palestine*. New York: Bantam Books, 1973.

Khadduri, Majdia D. *The Arab-Israeli Impasse*. Washington, D.C.: Robert B. Luce, 1968.

The Koran.

Laqueur, Walter. *Confrontation: The Middle East and World Politics*. New York: Quadrangle Books, 1974.

Larteguy, Jean. *The Walls of Israel*. New York: M. Evans & Co., 1968.

Mahan, Alfred T. *The Influence of Seapower upon History, 1660–1783*. New York: Hill & Wang, 1957.

Miller, Lt. (j.g.) F. C. "Those Storm-beaten Ships, Upon Which the Arab Armies Never Looked." *U.S. Naval Institute Proceedings* 101, No. 3/865 (March 1975): 18–25.

Miller, Martin J., Jr. "The Israeli Navy: 26 Years of Non-Peace." U.S. *Naval Institute Proceedings* 101, No. 2/864 (February 1975): 48–54.

Murphy, Charles J. V. "The Airlift that Saved Israel." *Reader's Digest* (July 1974), pp. 86–90.

O'Ballance, Edgar. *No Victor, No Vanquished: The Yom Kippur War.* London: Presidio Press, 1978.

Safran, Nadav. *From War to War: The Arab-Israeli Confrontation, 1948–1967.* New York: Pegasus, 1969.

Schmidt, Dana A. *Armageddon in the Middle East.* New York: J. Day, 1974.

Schweider, T. P. *Conflict Special Study #1: Arab-Israeli Armor 1973.* San Diego: Simulations Design Corp., 1975.

Shazli, Saad el. *The Crossing of the Suez.* San Francisco: American Mideast Research, 1980.

Sherman, Arnold. *When God Judged and Men Died.* New York: Bantam Books, 1973.

Simulations Publications, Inc. *Sinai.* New York: S.P.I., 1973.

Slonim, Shlomo. "Suez and the Soviets." U.S. *Naval Institute Proceedings* 101, No. 4/866 (April 1975): 36–41.

Smith, Terence. "Israelis West of Canal Find Burned-Out Zone." *The New York Times* (22 October 1973), p. 19.

Tanner, Henry. "Cairo Says Aim is Retaking Land." *The New York Times* (16 October 1973), p. 18.

Weeks, John. *Men Against Tanks.* New York: Mason/Charter, 1975.

Wragg, David W. *World's Air Forces.* New York: Hippocrene Books, 1971.

Young, Desmond. *Rommel: The Desert Fox.* New York: Berkley Publishing Corp., 1952.

MILITARY JOURNALS

Air Force, Armor, Armed Forces Journal, Army, Armies and Weapons, Aviation Week & Space Technology, Electronic Warfare, Infantry, International Defense Review, Marine Corps Gazette, Military Review, Naval War College Review, Seapower, Strategic Review.

GENERAL PERIODICALS

American Friends Service Committee, Business Week, Congressional Record, Current History, Department of State Bulletin, Economist, Foreign Affairs, Harper's

Magazine, London Sunday Times, Moves, Nation, The New Leader, New Republic, Newsweek, New York Times, Ramparts, Reader's Digest, Strategy & Tactics, Time, U.S. Code, Congressional and Administrative News, U.S. News & World Report, Wargamer's Digest, Washington Post.

SIMULATIONS

Bar-Lev, Conflict Game Company.
Jerusalem, Simulations Design Corporation.
Modern Battles, Sinai, and Sixth Fleet, Simulations Publications, Inc.

INDEX